The Breakthrough Experience

Arlene Wiede

Love

John Demartini

Hay House Titles of Related Interest

<u>Books</u>

Empowerment: *You Can Do, Be, and Have All Things,*
by John Randolph Price

Inner Peace for Busy People: *52 Simple Strategies for Transforming Your Life,*
by Joan Z. Borysenko, Ph.D.

Power vs. Force: *The Hidden Determinants of Human Behavior,*
by David R. Hawkins, M.D., Ph.D.

The Reconnection: *Heal Others, Heal Yourself,* by Dr. Eric Pearl

A Relationship for a Lifetime: *Everything You Need to Know to Create a Love
That Lasts,* by Kelly E. Johnson, M.D.

<u>Audio Programs</u>

How to Get What You Really, Really, Really, Really Want,
by Dr. Wayne W. Dyer and Deepak Chopra, M.D.

Improve Your Life Using the Wisdom of the Ages,
by Dr. Wayne W. Dyer

All of the above are available at your local bookstore,
or may be ordered by visiting:
Hay House USA: **www.hayhouse.com®**
Hay House Australia: **www.hayhouse.com.au**
Hay House UK: **www.hayhouse.co.uk**
Hay House South Africa: **orders@psdprom.co.za**
Hay House India: **www.hayhouseindia.co.in**

The Breakthrough Experience

A Revolutionary New Approach to Personal Transformation

DR. JOHN F. DEMARTINI

HAY HOUSE, INC.

Carlsbad, California

London • Sydney • Johannesburg

Vancouver • Hong Kong • New Delhi

Copyright © 2002 by John F. Demartini

Published and distributed in the United States by: Hay House, Inc.: www.hayhouse.com • *Published and distributed in Australia by:* Hay House Australia Pty. Ltd.: www.hayhouse.com. au • *Published and distributed in the United Kingdom by:* Hay House UK, Ltd.: www.hayhouse. co.uk • *Published and distributed in the Republic of South Africa by:* Hay House SA (Pty), Ltd.: orders@psdprom.co.za • *Distributed in Canada by:* Raincoast: www.raincoast.com • *Published in India by:* Hay House Publications (India) Pvt. Ltd.: www.hayhouseindia.co.in

Editorial Supervision: Jill Kramer • Design: Jenny Richards

Library of Congress Cataloging-in-Publication Data

Demartini, John F.
 The breakthrough experience : a revolutionary new approach to personal transformation
/ John F. Demartini.
  p. cm.
  ISBN 1-56170-885-2 (pbk.)
  1. Spiritual life. I. Title.

 BL624 .D3885 2002
 158.1—dc21

2001051860

ISBN 13: 978-1-56170-885-7
ISBN 10: 1-56170-885-2

09 08 07 06   11 10 9 8
1st printing, May 2002
8th printing, November 2006

Printed in the United States of America

Also by Dr. John F. Demartini

How to Make One Hell of a Profit and Still Get to Heaven

You Can Have an Amazing Life . . . in Just 60 Days!

Special Thanks

I want to thank Toni Robino for her assistance in my previous book, *Count Your Blessings*, and for her role as a creative catalyst in the genesis of this present volume.

A very special thank you to my friend and colleague, Timothy Marlowe, for his inspired work in transcribing, collating, and editing the presentations from which this book was drawn. Without his tireless commitment and understanding of universal principles, this would have been a very different book.

I offer many thanks to freelance editor Gail Fink, whose fine-tuning of this manuscript is greatly appreciated.

I send gratitude to all of the teachers and attendees of *The Breakthrough Experience*™, without whom this message would not be spreading so rapidly across the world.

Heartfelt thanks to my beautiful wife, Athena Starwoman, for her incredible intuition and cosmic vision.

And a final thank you to Dr. Paul C. Bragg, for his inspiration, his teachings, and the life-changing affirmation that he imparted to me in 1972.

Contents

Foreword

During the past 20 years of practicing psychiatry, I have studied with the finest teachers. Not only at Baylor College of Medicine in Texas, where I did my training, but all over the world, as I have traveled extensively to continue my studies. I have wanted to improve my ability to deal with the profound suffering of my patients. Over the years, I have found psychiatric programs that have gained great recognition across the country. I search, feeling like an archeologist looking for and connecting pieces of wisdom and understanding. I also had the desire not to be a "shrink," but on the contrary, I wanted to help my patients to "expand" conscious awareness. Through reading, I have gathered ideas and glimpsed great dimensions of consciousness. This search allowed me to have great opportunities to work with gifted "mind astronauts." The scientist in me wanted to go to space and experience the symmetry and order of the universe. How can I bring these concepts to planet Earth?

According to Mohandas K. Gandhi, if your wishes are pure, then they become true. At a certain point in my journey, I encountered the teachings of Dr. John F. Demartini. Finally, I had the language I had been searching for and the practical tools to make an extraordinary difference in people's lives. Dr. Demartini calls his method The Quantum Collapse Process. As a psychiatrist, I often refer to his method, combined with my medical expertise, as Quantum Collapse Therapy.

The Collapse Process allows individuals to be fully responsible for themselves and to experience their magnificence. It has been the greatest shift in paradigm that I have encountered. The Collapse Process is not about being better, improving, or changing; it is about true transformation. Each cell has a form. When the tissue is healthy, it is in perfect symmetry. The tissue is free of deformation or disease. Our thoughts, similar to these cells, get deformed with dysfunctional thoughts, feelings, or beliefs. The Collapse Process transforms thoughts, beliefs, and feelings that were once deformed or dysfunctional into thoughts that are in perfect symmetry and order. As we transform our thoughts, we transform our feelings and transform our life.

This book belongs to a new generation. It is a gift to the new millennium. The wisdom and inspiration and fresher vision are immeasurable. These teachings offer you a clearer and magnificent understanding of the powerful laws of the mind. Dr. Demartini provides Inspirational Guidance to manifest our Master Plan within the context of the purpose of our existence.

The uniqueness, originality, and genius of Dr. Demartini's ideas have already begun a revolutionary approach to psychiatric treatment. Over half of a century ago, the great Dr. Sigmund Freud talked about the unconscious and developed his techniques for understanding it. Now, Dr. Demartini's teaching allows individuals to experience and understand the wisdom not only of their unconscious minds, but also their consciousness and superconsciousness. Dr. Demartini's teachings have helped me with brilliant ideas and tools to help my patients become "Masters of their Destinies, not Victims of their Histories."

— Blanca Diez, M.D., P.A., Medical Director of the New Dimensions
    Day Treatment Program, Houston, Texas • *e-mail:* bdiezmd@aol.com

We Do Not Walk Alone

One night, a man dreamt that he walked along a shore
with the Divine Source of all things, and as they walked,
scenes from his life flashed across the sky above them.
Most of the time, he saw two sets of footprints in the sand
for each scene, but many times along the path there was
only one set of footprints, often at the very darkest and
saddest times, and the man was greatly troubled.

He turned to the figure beside him and said, "I looked for
you and tried to serve you all my days. I thought that you
would care for me in return, yet now I see that during
the most difficult times of my life, I was alone.
I don't understand why you would leave me
when I needed you most."

The Divine Intelligence replied, "My precious child,
you are always in my heart, and I would not desert
you in your times of trial and difficulty. When you
saw only one set of footprints in the sand,
it was then that I carried you."

— Mary Stevenson

It's a paradox, but those who seek God most are the ones who most deny God's presence. They go off on a quest to find divinity, and at the end, they look back and realize it was here all along. This book is the story of the quest for divine light, and it shows how science and religion have gone hand in hand down that path as they searched in their own ways for the same destination. It is about love, wisdom, and divine order, and how we have never been alone on this magnificent journey toward our destiny.

Introduction

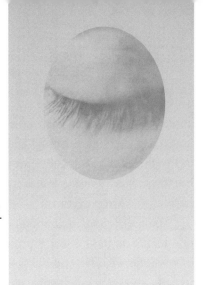

This book has been written to help you break through whatever barriers may be keeping you from experiencing your true and enlightened nature. It presents a completely accessible science and philosophy, and reveals and explores universal principles that underlie your very existence. Most important, this is an extremely real and practical manual for understanding why you live the way you do and how to transform your life into your highest vision.

What you're about to read is the synthesis of my 29 years of research and 24 years of clinical experience as a chiropractor, healer, and professional teacher. It is based on my two-day seminar program, The Breakthrough Experience™. While it would be impossible to include everything that happens during this extraordinary and intense course, I've blended its universal principles with autobiography; stimulating words from many of the great minds in history; and a host of true stories about ordinary people having extraordinary, astonishing, life-moving experiences.

The science is cutting edge, the philosophy is inspiring and daring, and the intermingling stories are all real. The exercises at the end of each chapter are designed to provide you with a personal experience of the profound and hidden truths underlying your life, and the affirmations and quotations are intended to awaken your true potential.

In the pages that follow, you will learn a formula for materializing your dreams, discover the secrets of opening your heart beyond anything you have imagined, find out how to increase your love and appreciation for every aspect of life, receive profound insights on how to create more fulfilling and caring relationships, reawaken your birthright as a true genius, transcend any fears and illusions surrounding the myth of death, and reconnect with your true mission and purpose for life on Earth.

You are about to embark on an experience that has never been put into this form before, and I promise that the time and effort devoted to it will be repaid a thousandfold. It is my sincere hope that this book will deeply touch and inspire you with respect to your own greatness and potential, and that it will reveal to you the magnificence of every single human soul. This is not just a book; it is what the title implies: an *experience*. I think you will find that it is impossible to go through it without being moved, challenged, and changed.

Thank you, and welcome to *The Breakthrough Experience.*

— **Dr. John F. Demartini**

Chapter One

The Essence of Life

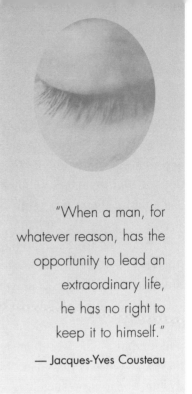

"When a man, for whatever reason, has the opportunity to lead an extraordinary life, he has no right to keep it to himself."

— Jacques-Yves Cousteau

I have a message I'd love to share that means so much to me. It is my mission and my service here on Earth. I want you to come on a journey with me—a journey using parts of my own life to illustrate the truth that every single one of us has greatness and immortal genius inside. No matter how we appear or what our circumstances are, everything that happens is directed toward waking us up to that gift and potential. We may have positive and negative opinions about the various people and events in our lives, but in truth, they all play a perfect role in unfolding our destiny and making us who we are.

The Breakthrough Experience began in 1989 when I was flying from Houston, Texas, to Quebec, Canada, to present a program to a group of health professionals. On the flight, I was meditating, and at about 30,000 feet, I had a vision. It came from my inner consciousness and revealed: "Breakthrough to Higher Power: The Vision, Inspiration, and Purpose Seminar." I saw not only an outline for the seminar, but many other details—even the number of people who were to attend.

Thousands of people in dozens of countries have since passed through the program on which you are about to embark, and their lives have been profoundly changed as a result of their insights and experiences. The vision of "The Breakthrough Experience," as I later titled it, was truly an inspiration. When you follow your inspirations and intuition, you grow in self-worth and potential, as well as toward your true capabilities. It's important to follow your vision, intuition, and inspiration so you can achieve what you're here to accomplish in life. Those inklings are messages; they are links to the highest source of wisdom available to you.

Before you finish this book, it's my goal to give you a glimpse and a feel for how magnificent you are. Due to the various beliefs and philosophies in the world, many people go through life thinking that they're less than perfect. They believe they're messed up or somehow dysfunctional, no matter how successful, famous, or beautiful they may be. There is even a psychological movement based on the myth of the dysfunctional family, but I have yet to find a family that wasn't balanced and functioning perfectly enough to give its members exactly what they needed to fulfill their lives—once the entire family was understood and probed into deeply.

With the ideas and tools I'll be presenting in this book, you'll realize that you are magnificent, and everything that has ever happened to you was vital to your becoming the unique being you are. I don't mean this in an optimistic, illusory, or Pollyannaish sense. In a deep and profound way, you will know how magnificent you are and how much you contribute to the world, just as you are now.

I travel extensively, and no matter where I go, and no matter which continent I step foot on, I've noticed a common theme among all people: Everyone wants to love and be loved, to appreciate and be appreciated, and everyone wants to live his or her dreams. There are certain laws that govern dreams, and if we follow those laws, we can fulfill our dreams. I've spent 29 years developing the science of love and appreciation, and now we can all apply it to make our dreams come true. It doesn't have to be hit-and-miss anymore. It's no longer a matter of luck or blind faith. There is now a *true science* of creating love and appreciation on planet Earth.

Science and Religion

Pseudoscience and pseudoreligion struggle and argue, but true science and true religion say the same thing. As Albert Einstein once said, "Science without religion is lame; religion without science is blind." Although some might argue that the mind is made of an intellectual component, and the soul consists of a revelatory or inspirational component, I intend to merge them together to give you an experience that synthesizes both. My goal is for you to open your heart wider than you may have ever done before, to allow you to get clearer about your purpose in life, to help you become more inspired about this magnificent universe we get to work in, and to enable your human mind to awaken to its divine birthright.

We've been given an extraordinary gift. Of all the places in the universe that we've explored, we've never come across anything more magnificent than the human body, brain, and spirit. Nothing is more amazing than the inspirations that come through that spirit to the brain, the body, and out into this world.

I remember sitting on the floor in my parents' house when I was 18 and reading *Discourse on Metaphysics* by the Western philosopher Gottfried W. Leibniz. He believed that humans are wise to acknowledge the loving intelligence of the universe. Although we sometimes personify this great intelligence as a deity and say it's omnipotent, omniscient, and omnipresent, we often don't perceive it in our individual daily experiences. When things are going our way, we say that our life is all part of this perfection, but when something doesn't go our way, we think, *Well, here's a little flaw in the perfection.*

As I read the first chapter and became introduced to what Leibniz called "divine perfection," I felt his depth of understanding and his certainty that there *was* a universal design, a hidden order, and an underlying magnificence to things. His words awoke tears of inspiration in me and I thought, *There has to be something significant here, and it's just a lack of our understanding that keeps us from acknowledging this hidden, divine order.*

Have you ever read or listened to something and gotten tears in your eyes and felt inspired? Those tears are an infallible clue that something meaningful and important for you is being revealed. Don't ignore these times—keep a log of those moments, those insights and tears, and you will find a story being told by your intuitive spirit, a story linked to your destiny. It's a gift from the part of you that knows, to the part of you that wonders. So write them down.

Leibniz's inspiring message touched my heart. There's an immortal part of us that *knows* the truth and a mortal part that *denies* it, and he awakened the immortal part in me. He left his imprint within my consciousness and put me on a quest to discover why so few people understand and acknowledge that beautiful order.

At the time, I thought, *I would love to discover a way to awaken the awareness of the divine order in people's lives, and the love in their hearts. What if it was possible to awaken them to the power that drives the evolution of life?*

As I went through college, I carried that dream with me. I studied everything I could about the universe. I loved cosmology (the study of the origin and structure of the universe) because it was like a modern form of the four great ancient questions of philosophy: *Who are we? Where do we come from? Why are we here?* and *Where are we going?* Cosmology was mind-expanding and absolutely fascinating. It led me into the world of astronomy, which took me into physics. Physics led me into the metaphysics of Aristotle, William James, and others, which launched me into theology. Theology then led me into mythology, which opened my eyes to anthropology. My investigations kept spreading until I eventually studied more than 200 different "ologies."

I began to realize that if I was going to study universal principles, I shouldn't limit myself to just the "ologies." I wanted to study *everything!* That seemed like a large quest, but I knew that "by the mile it's a pile, by the yard it's hard, by the inch it's a cinch!" If I just took it a little at a time, I could accomplish anything I felt called to do.

The more I investigated the principles of the universe, the more inspired and certain I became. I discovered some of the same laws and patterns underlying all the different fields—from the many arts and sciences, to the various religions and philosophies of life. These patterns stand the test of time. They awaken us to our truest and highest potential, and they are the foundation of The Breakthrough Experience.

Gratitude Is the Key

My mother told me when I was almost four years old, as she was putting me to bed one night, "Son, before you go to sleep tonight, make sure you count your blessings." Great truths are often hidden within such simple words.

When we see the underlying patterns and order in the universe, we come to an illuminating state of gratitude. Every time we're grateful for the extraordinary architectural creation called our being, our body, and our life, we take another step toward manifesting our greatest potential and fulfilling our true and ingenious destiny on this planet.

Those who are grateful have more blessings and fulfillment in life than those who do not. This is a simple principle, yet it has the power to change your life. Gratitude is the key to growth and fulfillment. If you were to give someone a gift and they just looked at it and then tossed it aside without thanks, would you be inclined to give them another? Of course not, and the universe responds just as you do. We're built on universal principles, and the universe behaves like us on a grander scale. The universe bestows its gifts where they're most appreciated. If you're not grateful for what you've been given, then why would the universe want to give you more?

> *"The hardest arithmetic to master is that*
> *which enables us to count our blessings."*
> — Eric Hoffer

I'm often asked, "What exactly is gratitude?" It's what you feel when you've attained perfectly balanced perception. It's what you experience when you see the perfect equilibrium or divine order in any area of your life. In Spanish it's called *gracias,* and in French it's called *merci,* but in English it's simply called *divine grace.*

Many people confuse gratitude with elation. They think that when they're elated about something and say, "Oh, I'm so thankful for that!" they're being grateful. But true gratitude actually has little to do with those temporary moments of happiness or elation. True gratitude is a quiet state of poise and inner calm where you're truly thankful, where you sense the divine order and wouldn't want anything to change.

Gratitude is a true prayer of thanksgiving, but there are two types of prayer. The first type is false prayer. It arises when you're dissatisfied with life and it often sounds something like, "Oh, Lord, this is all messed up. Please fix it!" The second type is true prayer. It arises when you recognize the order and perfection of what is and you're truly thankful for what has already been given. As a result, you receive even more gifts. To those who are grateful, more is given. To those who are not, more is taken away. Having gifts taken away as a result of ingratitude helps you wake up to the importance of being grateful.

Nothing has ever happened or can happen to you that is not a gift and a blessing, but it's difficult to be thankful until you find the hidden benefit in what may seem at first to be a negative event.

The Journey Begins

One of my most significant hidden blessings came to me in the first grade. I was a left-handed dyslexic, unable to read or comprehend, and my teacher knew little about learning disabilities. I started in the general class, was moved to a remedial reading class, and finally ended up in the "dunce class," where I sometimes had to sit in a corner and wear a conical dunce cap on my head. I felt ashamed, different, and rejected.

One day my teacher asked my parents to come to class. In front of me, she told them, "Mr. and Mrs. Demartini, your son has a learning disability. I'm afraid he will never read, write, or communicate normally. I wouldn't expect him to do much in life, and I don't think he'll go very far. If I were you, I would put him into sports." Although I didn't fully understand the significance of her words, I sensed my parents' uncertainty and concern.

I went into sports and eventually developed a real love for surfing. At the age of 14, I told my father, "I'm going to California to go surfing, Dad."

He looked me in the eye and sensed that I was sincere, and that no matter what he said, I was going to do it, because that was where I belonged. He asked me, "Are you capable of handling whatever happens? Are you willing to take whatever responsibilities come along?"

"Yes, I am."

He said, "I'm not going to fight you, son. You have my blessings." And he prepared a notarized letter saying, "My son is not a runaway. He's not a vagrant. He's a boy with a dream."

Years later, I found out that when my dad came back from World War II, he had hoped to go to California, but didn't. When he heard me say I was going to California, I believe his old dream came back to him and he thought, *I never made it, but I'm not going to stop you.*

So at the age of 14, I dropped out of school. My mom and dad gave me a ride to the freeway, lovingly said good-bye, and told me, "Go follow your dreams."

My First Mentor

From my hometown of Richmond, Texas, I set off hitchhiking toward California, and soon I arrived in El Paso. I was walking through town on my way to the West Coast, moving down a sidewalk with no place to go but straight ahead, when I saw three cowboys ahead of me.

Back in the '60s, cowboys and surfers didn't get along. An underlying war existed between the shorthaired rednecks and longhaired "white-necks." As I walked down that sidewalk with my backpack, surfboard, long hair, and headband, I knew I was about to be confronted. As I approached, they lined up across the sidewalk and stood there with their thumbs in their belts. They weren't going to let me through.

I was thinking, *Oh, God, what am I gonna do?,* when all of a sudden, for the very first time, my inner voice spoke to me. It told me to . . . bark! Now, that may not have been the most inspired inner voice, but it was the only one I had. It said to bark, so I just went along with it and started to bark, "Ruff! Ruff! Raaarrrruff!" and lo and behold, the cowboys got out of my way.

For the first time, I learned that if I trusted my intuition, amazing things would happen.

I growled my way through the three men, still going, "Raaarrufff! Ruff! Ruff! RRRRUUUFFF!" and they moved out of the way, probably thinking, *This kid is nuts!* As I walked safely past the three cowboys, I felt like I had just come out of a trance. I slowly turned away from them as I came up to the corner, and there, leaning on a lamppost, roaring with laughter, was a baldheaded old bum in his 60s with about four days worth of stubble. He was laughing so hard he had to hang on to the lamppost to hold himself up.

"Sonny," he said, "that's the funniest dang thing I've ever seen. You took care of them cowpokes like a pro!" He put his hand on my shoulder and walked me down the street.

He said, "Can I buy you a cup of coffee?"

I said, "No, sir, I don't drink coffee."

"Well, can I buy you a Coke?"

"Well, yes, sir!"

We walked up to a little malt shop with swivel stools along the counter. Inside, we sat down and he asked, "So where ya headed, sonny?"

"I'm going to California."

"Are you a runaway?"

"No, my parents gave me a ride to the freeway."

"You dropped out of school?"

"Well, yeah. I was told I would never read, write, or communicate, so I just went into sports. I'm going to California to be a surfer."

He said, "Are you finished with your Coke?"

"Yep."

"You follow me, young boy."

So I followed this scruffy man, and he took me a few blocks down the street, and then a few blocks more, and he led me through the front doors of the downtown El Paso library.

He pointed to a spot on the floor. "Put your stuff down here, it'll be safe," and we walked through the library, where he sat me down at a table.

"Sit down, young boy. Sit down and I'll be right back," and off he went into the bookshelves.

In a few minutes, he came back with a couple of books and sat down next to me. "There are two things I want to teach you, young man, two things I don't want you to ever forget. You promise?"

"Yes, sir, I do."

My newfound mentor said, "Number one, young fella, is never judge a book by its cover."

"Yes, sir."

"Because you probably think I'm a bum. But let me tell you a little secret. I'm one of the wealthiest men in America. I come from the Northeast, and I have every single thing that money has ever been able to buy—the cars, the planes, the houses. A year ago, someone very dear to me passed away, and when she went, I reflected on my life and thought, *I have everything except one experience. What's it like to have nothing, and to live on the streets?*

"So I made a commitment to travel around America and go from city to city, with nothing, just to have that experience before I died. So, son, don't you ever judge a book by its cover, because it will fool you."

Then he grabbed my right hand and pulled it forward and set it on top of the two books he had put there. They were the works of Aristotle and Plato, and he said with such intensity and clarity that I've never forgotten it: "You learn how to read, boy. You learn how to read, 'cause there's only two things that the world can't take away from you: your love and your wisdom. They can take away your loved ones, they can take away your money, they can take away just about everything, but they can't take away your love and wisdom. You remember that, boy."

I said, "Yes, sir, I will."

And then he walked me over a few blocks and sent me on my way to California. To this day I have never forgotten his message, and it has become the core of The Breakthrough Experience: Love and wisdom are the essence of life.

Divine Order

Everything that happens is a vital part of the divine order that Leibniz, Einstein, St. Augustine, and most of the great minds understood. Even the most terrible events always contain hidden blessings. The masters know this great truth and remain undisturbed by events, while those of lesser wisdom swing from elation to depression as they move through positive and negative experiences on their way to understanding.

Childhood deprivation is often the source of adult dreams and aspirations. So often childhood illnesses create the great healer or athlete. Those who think they weren't loved seek to share love wholeheartedly for the rest of their lives. Those who felt unworthy develop a powerful drive to contribute to the world and feel worthwhile. Those who lived in poverty go on to amass great wealth. Perceived voids create values; we are programmed to seek whatever we think is missing the most.

Although I didn't know it at the time, the "tragedy" of my learning difficulties and dyslexia set me free to follow my dreams and meet extraordinary people who would guide my life. I discovered an irresistible desire to achieve what I was told I would never do. I was told I would never read, write, or communicate, yet today I spend more than 300 days a year traveling the world doing exactly that.

Wisdom is the instantaneous recognition that a crisis is a blessing, and even greater wisdom recognizes that blessings can also trigger a crisis. When we truly understand that, we're less likely to be upset about difficulties or elated about opportunities; we remain centered no matter what happens around us. That is one of the secrets of self-mastery.

When you know that bad things aren't so terrible and good things aren't so terrific, you can be quietly grateful for whatever occurs. Balance is neither pessimism nor optimism. It doesn't lean to one side or the other, but sits poised in the middle. It is "gratefulism," and that is both wisdom and true power. All things are balanced, and when you know it, you remain true to yourself rather than being driven by your hopes and fears. You stay present on your path.

When you buy into the fantasy of better and worse, seeking the illusion of greener pastures, you're never present, or satisfied with your life the way it is. You think, *Someday I'll find a way to let my wife and children know how much I really love them. Someday when things are better, I'll start that business, take that trip, or write that book.* You live on Someday Isle, which doesn't exist.

Napoleon Hill, the author of *Think and Grow Rich,* once said, "Don't look for opportunities in the far distances of space and time, but embrace them right where you are, because where you are already has the perfection and the balance." Right this minute you have everything you need to fulfill your life.

One of the objectives of The Breakthrough Experience is to help you see through your inner eye the balance that already exists. When you're truly grateful, you have simply woken up to it.

The Great Discovery

In my search for the principles underlying human existence and consciousness, I came upon what I call The Great Discovery™: At any moment of your life, you will never be put down without being lifted up, nor lifted up without being put down. Positive and negative, good and bad, support and challenge, peace and war—all come together in pairs. They are simultaneous and perfectly balanced, and that is what makes up the divine order.

At first that may seem somewhat less than startling. But when it sinks in, you'll realize that it's truly an amazing understanding. If you ever see one side without the other, you're living in an illusion. Stop right now and think about your life. Find a moment where you were criticized, put down, or humiliated. Isolate the exact moment in space and time and the exact individual or group. Once you pinpoint this moment of humiliation, look again, and you'll find that at *exactly* the same time you were being put down, either you or somebody else was lifting you up and praising you. In addition, any time you were put up on a pedestal, that was the very moment somebody brought you down and put you in the pit. Wisdom is the acknowledgment that both sides occur equally and simultaneously.

Each of us lives in duality; we are all bipolar people. We have a part that lifts us up and another that puts us down. We praise and criticize ourselves. Nobody will ever put us up or down as much as we do, because no one will ever think as much or as intensely about us as we think about ourselves. When somebody reacts to us, they're merely reflecting a repressed part of us. No one ever victimizes us; they just *reflect* us.

I once consulted for a doctor in Los Angeles who said, "I need some help, John. I'm running into a series of patients who say there's no way they can possibly commit to the necessary care for that long."

"So what are your responses?" I asked him.

"Well, that's it. I don't have responses, and I keep blowing it. I'm calling you to get some ideas."

He was giving his patients a plan of action for their health care, which had worked fine for months, but all of a sudden he was getting this objection over and over again. I know the world is a mirror, so I just asked him, "Where are *you* holding back from committing that long?"

He had just been talked into getting married. He loved the lady and a part of him definitely wanted to get married, but he was frightened of the commitment because he'd been through it before. The week he agreed to marry her, he started getting this objection from his patients. His fear was financial, so when I helped him work out a prenuptial agreement, his fear of marriage evaporated and his clients soon stopped refusing to commit. His financial "problem" helped him organize and break through his relationship fears and open his heart to the woman he loved.

People treat you exactly the way you unconsciously treat yourself. Their outer mannerisms toward you reflect your inner mannerisms, so one of the most powerful ways to transform your life is to become consciously aware of your beliefs and feelings about yourself. Most people go through life completely oblivious. They have high moments and low moments and swing through their emotions, but don't see the balanced and divine order, and how they're constantly surrounded by love. My objective is to have you become aware that you're surrounded by magnificent love every moment of your life.

True Love

True love emerges from a state of emotional balance. One of the purposes of having a partner is to maintain a loving equilibrium. If one partner is manic and up, the other partner helps bring them back down into balance. If one is down and depressed, the other will help lift them up. If one partner becomes cocky, the other brings them down. If one becomes deflated, the other helps them up. That's how relationships work. This balancing act maintains the divine order, or true love.

I used to come home from my office after a "big day"—I'd see a pile of patients, provide a load of service, and make lots of money. I'd drive home in my Jaguar all cocky and elated, thinking, *Oh, wow, what a day! Anybody want to touch me for luck?*

I'd sail home and . . . *boom!* Slam dunk. "Where have you been? We were supposed to go out to dinner an hour ago. Did you pick up what I asked you for? Who do you think you are, anyway?" I would come down with a crash because I didn't understand how that was actually great love.

My first, immature response was, "Well, thanks very much. I was so up and positive and I had such a great day. How come you're putting me down? I work so hard and you don't support me. Everybody else sees how great I am. What's wrong with you?"

And do you know what would happen? No intimate activity for a week. I would get humbled because *we're not here to be right, we're here to be love.* These two sides make up true love. They create the balance. I was surrounded by love, but I was addicted to the pleasure at work and resentful of the balancing pain at home. I eventually realized that every time I came home cocky, I wasn't present with my family. And if I wasn't present and in love with my family, the slam dunk returned me to being present with them. But if I came home really depressed, there was my wife, lifting me up.

I realized that if I wanted to come home and find love there, I'd better not be elated or cocky. So on the drive home I would think, *All right, what patient did I forget to call? What paperwork did I forget to do? Who did I not give my best quality service to?* I would humble myself and not walk into the house until I felt centered and present.

Like any true science that's reproducible, if you do that, you will repeatedly have a loving partner at home. It's absolutely amazing. You literally have the power to change the state of your partner, from a distance, by going into the state of balanced love. When you have true love, you see the balance all around you. When you have a one-sided emotion, you get the other side to center you and bring you back to true and balanced love. This is the divine order at work.

The moment you realize this balance and observe the perfect equilibrium around you, you become liberated. You know that the world is perfectly balanced, both within and without. Only then are you able to manage your own life and no longer be controlled by praise and blame. You begin to forge your own destiny and allow the enlightened part of you to direct your life, rather than let yourself be run by the part of you that hopes and fears.

If you would love to be the director of your own life, you must equilibrate your perceptions and emotions. By equilibration, I don't mean indifference or apathy; I mean a point of inner balance and poise that goes beyond emotional extremes. The heart opens only when the mind becomes consciously equilibrated, while imbalanced emotions close it down. That's why St. Augustine emphasized that "the will of God is equilibrium." God wants you to open your heart to yourself and recognize that you are a part of that divinity—beyond any opinions of grandeur, unworthiness, and doubting fears.

When the will of humans attunes to the balanced will of God, the heart communes with divinity. As human beings, our job is to become acutely aware of the life dynamics that are doing everything they can to equilibrate us and make us aware of this truth. When we begin to see the balance everywhere, we wake up to the possibility that maybe there's a hidden order and intelligence behind it all.

Love is made up of two sides: support and challenge. We're required to experience both sides equally, and live in this world of duality until we can see the magnificence of their underlying balance. Were you aware that supporting someone can make them weak and dependent, and that challenging them can make them strong and independent? We judge ourselves harshly when we feel we've been mean to someone, but that's because we haven't seen the balance. Because of the divine order, the very person we were mean to received kindness from someone else at exactly the same time. Our meanness made them more independent, and the other person's kindness made them more dependent. You wouldn't believe how many times I've seen a child being challenged by the father, while the mother was supportive, and vice versa. The more gentle and lenient one parent was, the more rough and strict the other was. The softer one was, the harder the other got, and the two together made up the balance of love.

A child requires both support and challenge in perfect equilibrium. If one parent plays one side, the other parent will play the other. If not, the brother or sister will play it, or the kid down the street will beat them up. They won't escape whatever it takes to equilibrate them. Look at your own life to see the truth of what I'm saying. Can you think of times when you received both praise and reprimand in equilibrium? You can't escape it. If you had nothing but challenge right from birth, you wouldn't survive your family. If you had nothing but support from your family, you wouldn't survive when you went out into the world.

Nature won't allow anything but equilibrium. Have you ever wondered why some of the most famous rock stars and movie stars commit suicide, overdose, or self-destruct? Their suicidal tendencies or suicide attempts are often compensatory reactions to having other people build them up so high that they imagine themselves invincible. Because praise and blame are equilibrated, anyone who buys into the illusion that they're greater than they really are will also blame themselves and self-destruct for not being able to measure up to their fantasy. Strange as it may seem, critics and the tabloids actually help keep celebrities alive by balancing all the praise and adulation they receive.

One of the greatest illusions people fall into is the search for pleasure without pain, praise without reprimand, or nice without mean. Looking for elusive, one-sided events in a two-sided universe is the root of people's so-called suffering. When you embrace the balance and the truth, love surrounds you. You can't escape true love. You can't run from it. There's nowhere to go. When you understand this truth, your fears and guilt can evaporate, and you can begin to dance with your life.

The Master Dance

I once lived in a house overlooking the beach near Del Mar, California. One day I walked into a health-food store for a carrot juice and overheard a gentleman talking about philosophy. I couldn't resist the opportunity, so I sat down with him for a discussion. He told me he was a master of martial arts, had trained many Hollywood movie stars, and also studied philosophy. After our lengthy discussion, he asked me if I would be willing to share more of my philosophy with him in exchange for some martial arts lessons. Of course I accepted, and he came over to my home.

I took him into my family's big, glass-walled room overlooking the beach and asked him, "All right, what do I do?"

He said, "Okay, here's the first lesson. I want you to do whatever you can to attack me. Try to kill me."

I thought, *Hmm, the first lesson and he wants me to kill him. Okaaay.*

So I tried to punch him, and immediately, with just two fingers, he grabbed my arm and twisted me off balance, leaned me backwards, kissed me on the cheek, and put me back on my feet. With two fingers!

He said, "Try again."

I thought, *All right, I'm going to try kicking him*, but as I kicked, he stepped aside and used the same two fingers to lift up my foot, throw me off balance, and kiss me on the cheek. The next time I tried a spinning kick, but he just guided my leg on past and kissed me on the cheek again. No matter what I did, I couldn't touch him, and eventually I started to laugh.

I stood back, sweating and out of breath, and asked him, "Okay, what's the lesson here?"

He said, "Here is your first lesson. To a master, there is no such thing as attacks, only invitations to dance. But to a neophyte, because they're unsure, they always perceive themselves to be the victim of attacks. Anything they're not prepared for will be interpreted as a danger, and it will run their lives. But anything that they can see as having a perfect balance of yin and yang, they will not react to. Masters act wisely upon such things, and they make them invitations to dance."

This gentleman didn't feel threatened by anything I could do because he had already prepared himself for every possibility. He stayed poised and present no matter what I did, and turned my attempts at deadly combat into a graceful dance. He was educational as well as entertaining to watch.

If we can understand and embrace everything that comes our way in the same spirit as this gentleman, knowing that it is not an attack, but an opportunity to refine and expand ourselves, we can turn our lives into the same masterful dance. For most of us, conflict is less physical and more verbal and mental, but the same principle applies. You're not present when you become distracted by the emotions of praise and reprimand, are you? When somebody lifts you up or puts you down, if you buy into their one-sided illusion, they can run your life. The second you allow yourself to get elated or depressed about other people's perceptions of you, or even your own illusory perceptions of yourself, you become disempowered. You cannot express your genius to its fullest while you're caught in that state. But the second you bring your mind to balanced awareness, you have the power of divinity working through you.

The next time someone puts you down, immediately look for the balancing opposite and say to yourself, "Ah, thank you! I was just being cocky and elated about something, and I was also being praised and built up, so I see why I've brought you into my life at this moment." If you can be thankful to them for helping you remain poised, you're on your way to becoming a master. If every time a crisis struck, you trained yourself to immediately look for the blessing and opportunity that certainly exists, you could dance with your life.

> *"If I had only one prayer, it would be, 'Thank you.'"*
> — Meister Eckhart

When you open your heart to Divine Intelligence, miracles happen in your life. Miracles are nothing but natural laws put into action by beings who understand their application. When you're poised and centered, you have power. You become like a Jedi knight and The Force is with you. Not because you want to gain control, but because you honor yourself and your life enough to embrace it all, the highs and lows are in perfect balance.

The purpose of The Breakthrough Experience is to assist you when you feel ready to honor your true nature and to shine. Shall we begin?

Many of the chapters in this book include exercises similar to the ones below. I urge you to give yourself the gift of completing each exercise before proceeding to the next chapter. They are a crucial part of The Breakthrough Experience, so take as much time as you need before moving on.

After the exercises, you'll find a list of affirmations called "Words of Wisdom and Power." Read these affirmations at least three times daily, concentrate on their significance, and feel them as they begin to take root in your heart and mind.

Exercise 1

Think of a moment in your life when you were criticized, put down, repressed, or told you were no good. It's important to identify the details: Exactly when, where, and by whom did this occur? Then remember who was lifting you up, praising and putting you on a pedestal, at that *exact* split second. Write them both down and identify their balance.

Over the days and weeks to come, begin scanning back over your entire life and equilibrate every lopsided word of criticism or praise you can remember. Love is two-sided. When you deeply understand this great truth, you get to be surrounded by love every minute of your life.

Exercise 2

Before you go to sleep tonight, lie comfortably in your bed and begin giving thanks inwardly. Remember everyone who helped you today. Call up their image in your mind's eye and thank them for their support or challenge, niceness or meanness, or simply their presence in your life. Identify what they were teaching you and how and what they were balancing.

Continue until you feel great gratitude for your day—until you see that both sides are perfectly balanced and both are love. Going to sleep with a grateful, open heart is a powerful healing practice. Your dreams will become more inspiring, and you will awaken in the morning with a lighter state of mind.

Words of Wisdom and Power

- *I am magnificent just the way I am.*
- *I listen to my immortal nature, and it knows.*
- *My true nature is love and wisdom. Wisdom is the instantaneous recognition that crisis is a blessing.*
- *Life is a gift. Thank you.*

Chapter Two

Lighten Up

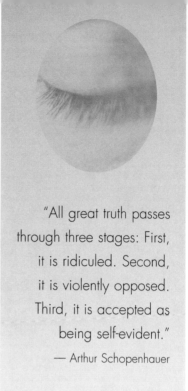

"All great truth passes through three stages: First, it is ridiculed. Second, it is violently opposed. Third, it is accepted as being self-evident."

— Arthur Schopenhauer

Did you know that your true nature, underneath all of your hopes, fears, thoughts, and feelings, is nothing but love and light? The universe has an inherent balance and order whose expression is this love and light. You have unlimited access to a boundless energy, the same energy that permeates all life—from the core of our radiant star to the center of a crimson rose. This universal order of love and light resides in the heart of all things, including *your* heart, and it opens up to you the minute you unlock it with the key of gratitude.

Once you recognize and attune with your Divine Source by balancing your mind, you have access to an infinite energy. This isn't just a metaphor or wishful New Age fantasy. It's as real as the sunrise and as solid as the book you hold right now, because everything *is* energy. This chapter is about how to access that infinite energy. Since command of any discipline lies in the mastery of its details, this chapter may be the most challenging as well as the most rewarding.

Recurring Themes

After passing my GED, and then taking entrance exams to get into college, at the age of 20 I found myself living in a dormitory with a bunch of physicists. I was rooming with a brilliant young man from Taiwan who dreamed of receiving a Nobel Prize. We would stay up until four in the morning trying to answer the questions at the cutting edge of physics and cosmology. We challenged each other to come up with more comprehensive theories than the Big Bang and Unified Field theories. I set out on a quest to know the essence of life and its energy source, as well as universal laws. I was driven to explore the mysteries surrounding energy, and to discover the secret of *consciousness*. Was it a science? Was it mysticism? Was it both? Little did I know the impact this quest would have on my life.

I discovered in my studies of physics, metaphysics, and theology that the theme of *light* kept recurring. The Bible says that God called forth heaven and earth with the words *fiat lux,* "Let there be light." The Old Masters painted holy beings with halos of light around their heads. Physicists and astronomers used light as the source and great measurer of phenomena. I wondered at the time, *Is it possible that visible light and spiritual light are the same thing? Could the same universal laws govern both?*

I noticed another recurring theme in physics: collapsing wave functions. Every atom or subatomic particle could function as a wave and also be reduced to mathematical equations involving spin, rotation, and other quantum numbers. When two complementary particles (those of equal yet opposite mass and opposite charge, such as matter and antimatter) are brought together, they annihilate each other and birth *light*. But when, in turn, they are simultaneously generated *from* light, one seems to disappear. This instantaneous disappearance is called "collapsing its wave function."

Then I came across the work of the world-famous physicist

Freeman Dyson, who presently teaches at the Institute for Advanced Study in Princeton, New Jersey. He was quoted in a 1993 *Scientific American* magazine article as saying, "No universe with intelligence is pointless . . . intelligence could persist for eternity—perhaps in the form of a cloud of charged particles (of light)—through shrewd conservation of energy."

If consciousness was somehow a cloud of charged particles of light, I wondered what that meant for humanity. Eventually I discovered that the mysteries of mind and the physics of light were related through the collapsing of full quantum-wave functions. The long-term result became The Quantum Collapse Process™, which is now the core of The Breakthrough Experience. By the end of this book, when you've had a chance to learn the foundations of this process and test it out for yourself, you will have a personal experience of its truth.

The next few chapters include some important fundamentals to prepare you for The Quantum Collapse Process. When you get to Chapter 9 and follow the instructions to the letter, you will experience this love and light. At that moment, these principles won't be just theories or opinions; they will become an integral part of how you experience and look at life. Once you experience a Collapse, the love won't be forgotten.

Being Here Now

As stated previously, when two complementary particles—or those with equal but opposite charges, spins, and masses—are brought together, they annihilate each other and birth light. In human consciousness, when two complementary emotions or those with equal but opposite charges (such as elation and depression or happiness and sadness), spin (forward and backward in time), and masses (burdening emotional distractions) are brought together and synthesized into perfect balance, the emotions annihilate each other and birth the feeling of love and light. Light and love are two aspects of the same phenomenon.

All positive and negative particles in the universe are created simultaneously, in perfect one-to-one balance, but your senses misperceive local imbalances and can mislead you. Every time you splinter yourself into positive and negative emotions, you scatter your light, dissipate your energy potential, and disempower your true and centered being. In this way, you separate yourself into past and future, and you're no longer present. When you bring your perceptions back into balance and become aware of how things truly *are*, you reverse the process. The past and future disappear in an all-encompassing state of loving presence. In the state of love, extraordinary things can happen.

You might ask, "How is that possible?" As long as you're attuned to your bodily senses, you're subject to space and time, because that's where your body lives. Time consists of both future and past, neither of which can ever be in the *now*. The past holds memory, is emotionally based, and is dominated by the emotion labeled *guilt*. The future holds imagination, is also emotionally based, and is dominated by the emotion labeled *fear*. The loving essence of your true spirit is spaceless and timeless *presence*. Anytime you experience a future or past emotion, you dissipate your potential energy into a kinetic motion. But in a state of presence and love, you reintegrate your kinetic energy and birth a new quantum of creative potential. The purpose of this book is to help you take your imbalanced emotions and reintegrate them back into the enlightening potentiality of true love.

Would you love to be in a place, but at the same time *not* be in that place? Would you love to have an entire room disappear except for the person you love? What if you had a chance to see someone who died 20 years ago and tell them how much you loved them? What if the person you *despised* or avoided for 20 or 30 years suddenly appeared next to you and you opened your heart to them; embraced, thanked, and loved them; and were set free from any emotional bondage or baggage? These are just a few of the experiences people report upon completing The Quantum Collapse Process.

Mothers and Fathers

Sometime ago, I presented The Breakthrough Experience in Los Angeles. In the audience was a beautiful lady (whom I'll call Jane) who had been given up by her Spanish mother and raised by a Frenchwoman. Jane did The Quantum Collapse Process on her birth mother, and upon completion, I asked her who in the room reminded her of her biological mother. She looked around the room and chose a middle-aged woman with asthma who was sitting by the outside door to get some fresh air. Jane spoke to this lady in Spanish, which was her original language, and then the woman started saying things that Jane's birth mother had said when she was a young girl, and the woman even somehow knew to call Jane by her nickname.

Afterward, the "surrogate mother" asked me, "How did I know her nickname? How did I know to say that? I felt like something was almost speaking through me and directed me on what to say. It was strange. It was as if I became her birth mother for a few moments."

When Jane finished that Collapse, I said, "So what about your stepmother? What is in the way of loving her?" We worked a little longer on her Collapse and balanced out any remaining imbalanced perceptions or emotions about her adoptive stepmother. I then asked her, "Who here reminds you now of your stepmother?"

Jane looked around the room and stopped at the same woman and said, "It's her again."

Astonishingly, this lady was trilingual. Now in the role of the stepmother, she spoke French and used the very words Jane's stepmother would have uttered. It was so real to both women that they conversed as if they'd never been apart.

Afterward, the surrogate mother returned to her chair, sat back comfortably, and had a new realization: Her asthma had momentarily cleared due to the impact of exchanging such deep love. Can you guess what had happened in her life? She had given away one of her daughters, and her emotions about it were partly the cause of her asthma! Psychosomatically, asthma results from frustration and anxiety associated with some kind of perceived loss, and also with feeling unworthy to live. The woman playing the role of both mothers then had the opportunity to clear her emotions about her lost daughter by doing her own Collapse. She had carried this emotion as pain and illness in her body since she was a young mother.

The serendipity and synchronicity of the people who attend The Breakthrough Experience seminars is quite profound and certainly no mistake. What happened with Jane was a beautiful experience, and it illustrates that when you love, the person becomes present with you and appears.

If it sounds way out or simply impossible, I say this now: My solemn promise to you is that I won't present anything here that isn't true, that hasn't been tested and experienced by hundreds and thousands of people. If anything, I will *under*state what is possible, and let you experience it for yourself. One of the most profound things you will ever experience is a true open heart in the presence of the one you love. It doesn't matter if they're alive or dead—there is a parallel spiritual world; and your loved ones, wherever they are, will be there with you.

Tough-Love Science

So let us now look at the phenomenon of people appearing. Pat yourself on your shoulder and feel the flesh under your hand. The physical body you just touched appears to be solid, but as a whole, it can be broken down into *systems* such as the nervous system, cardio-vascular system, and muscular system. Systems can be further broken down into *organs* such as the brain, stomach, and lungs. Organs are composed of *tissues* that are made up of *cells*, then *molecules*, then *atoms*, and then *subatomic particles*. Quantum physicists now know that all subatomic particles such as protons, electrons, neutrons, quarks, and mesons are all actually waves.

Your idea of having a solid physical body is an illusion of your senses. Your body is made up of nothing but electromagnetically res-onant waves. Most of your body is empty space that contains minute fields of vibrating waves. You are a vibrating system. You have prob-ably even said, "I'm picking up strange vibes today," or "Man, I don't like his vibes." You are made of pure vibrating light waves, which physicists call *quanta*.

I'm going to make you think a little bit here, but bear with me. Nothing of value comes without a price.

A quantum light wave is composed of peaks and troughs, or pos-itive and negative phases. Similarly, you are composed of peaks and troughs, or positive and negative *emotions*. The peak and trough phases correspond to the highs and lows of your consciousness; the same laws govern both. The positive phases of light waves are called *positrons*. The negative phases are called *electrons*. Neither of those phases by themselves is light; they are charged particles materialized in space and time. They each have mass, and participate in what is called *density*. If a complete light wave represented truth, then the positive or negative phases alone would represent only half-truths.

When positive and negative phases join together in perfect bal-ance, they birth *light*. Light doesn't move through space as a contin-uous bright streak; it pops in and out of existence as it jumps from one full wave, or quantum, to the next. In between the points of light (photons) are the positive and negative half-quantum particles (positrons and electrons). That's what a quantum leap is: a jump from one radiant state of illumination to the next.

Now you're probably wondering, *Where is this guy going with all of this physics stuff? Why is he talking about such abstract things?*

I'm talking about your *being,* your physical nature, as vibration. There are laws that govern those vibrations. When you apply those laws, you can understand what happens in life, and understanding is crucial to your illumination experience. Some physicists have said that the matter composing your physical body consists of frozen, condensed, and cooled light, and they're accurate. Actually, it's *all* light, all vibration, all spirit.

We're prepared to acknowledge these principles and laws in the physical world and assume they don't apply to the world of the mind, but our consciousness works in the same way that light does. Have you ever been cocky and elated about some part of your life, your finances, your career or relationship, and had something happen right at that moment to humble you? That's not mistake or error; it's exactly the way the universe makes sure you learn love. The second you see more positives than negatives, you attract a situation where you see more negatives than positives to get them back in balance.

There is a symmetry law in quantum physics that excludes any isolated half-quantum state (positron). There seems to always be an anti-half-quantum state (electron) somewhere in the universe to balance it. All phenomena are universally full-quantum. Looking at that law, I thought, *That implies there must be no such thing as happiness without sadness, or sadness without happiness.* That's a big jump, so I clinically explored this principle and interacted with thousands of people only to find it true.

Originally when somebody said, "I'm happy!" I would buy into it. But after my exploration, I realized that in every case, they were both sad *and* happy. When someone said they were sad, they were really playing a role. They were comparing their lives to a fantasy of what they thought it should be, and *that's* where their happiness was.

It was hidden in their virtual reality. But if I took them through The Quantum Collapse Process and merged the two emotional phases together, both disappeared and grateful love and light were birthed.

When I said that at a program in Mexico, a lady stood up and said, "I don't quite understand this because I'm a very happy person. I've always been happy, and in fact, I can't think of a time when I've been sad in my entire life."

I asked her, "And are the people around you sad because of that?" She said, "Well, I always try to cheer them up."

She couldn't stand to see sadness in others because she was repressing her own sadness. We later learned that she had been very ill recently. She had kidney, lung, and stomach problems, and had even had part of an organ removed. Her negativity went into her body and manifested as illness, and she hadn't realized the price she was paying for her so-called constant happiness.

Anytime you perceive a positive without a negative, you're drawn into a positive emotion; whenever you perceive a negative without a positive, you're drawn into a negative emotion; and both are lower-frequency (kinetic energy) states that dissipate your potential and run your life. Right in the middle between positive and negative emotions, between like and dislike, is the core of human experience, and it is nothing other than *love*. True love is a synthesis of the two aspects of one wave, and one full wave is light, which can also be called "love." Love is a full-quantum state. Physicists know that a full-quantum state is massless, chargeless, spaceless, and timeless, which by definition is spiritual and unconditional.

Consciousness is light, and it comes in full-quantum states. God is full-quantum light.

People have different definitions of *love,* but I'm defining it as "the synthesis or perfect blending of all dualistic perceptions, the summation of all polarities." When happiness and sadness are synthesized, they make love. Like and dislike, positive and negative, pain and pleasure, electron and positron—all dualities, when totally synthesized, are love. No matter what "ology" you investigate, they all lead to the same essence: love, the unified field theory that permeates every human being and links us all.

"Without love there is no life,
and the life is of such a quality as is the love."
— Emanuel Swedenborg

When you're in the illusion of one-sided positive or negative experiences, you automatically attract the opposite side to balance you. When you acknowledge life's perfection by embracing both of its sides, you experience unconditional love. An infallible sign that the two sides have become integrated is tears of love, and they appear again and again throughout this book. They aren't tears of happiness or sadness; they are tears of love and inspiration, and it is physiologically impossible to come to a point of synthesis without them. The bigger and more widely separated the emotional charges, the more intense and profound the tears are when those charges are synthesized.

It takes both positive and negative particles in perfect synthesis to create light, and in exactly the same way, you need both sides of every event to hone you in on your true nature, which is also light. The light in the center is unconditional love; the emotional or particle waves are conditional love. They draw in their opposite side, which you need to bring you back to the center, but it's *all* love.

Mother Love

Conventional wisdom believes that love is only the nice, positive, and supportive side of the equation, but the synthesis of the two halves is a vastly more powerful noumenon,[1] which I call love. This universal principle applies in the most extreme situations and circumstances, not just in minor negatives and difficulties.

I once had the opportunity to work with an intense man who, when I asked him who in his life he had the biggest emotional charge on, said, "Well, I guess that would be my mother. If she were alive, I'd put out a contract to have her killed."

His mother had been a drug-addicted prostitute who had tried to kill him not once, but many times, and eventually committed suicide. He'd been taken away from her while still very young, and had been placed in an orphanage, then a foster home. Later he visited his old neighborhood and checked hospital and other records. He had recalled only a few of the incidents, but discovered an almost unbelievable history of so-called violence. He found that she had stabbed and poisoned him, left him outside unclothed in the winter, tried to smother him, and had done just about everything you could imagine to take his life, but he had survived it all.

His mother had two sides, the side that wanted him disposed of, and the side that didn't. I set out to help him find the other side of her love, and at first he just looked at me as if I were crazy. Since I know the full-quantum principle, we just kept digging. I asked him to recall where he had done exactly what he accused her of, in someone else's perception, and he flat-out denied that he could be anything like her. With perseverance, we unearthed every single thing he resented her for in his own life, though in his own expressed forms.

This man was a prosecution lawyer who'd never lost a case. He had once prosecuted his best friend who felt stabbed in the back by him, and their relationship was poisoned. Defense lawyers felt overwhelmed and smothered by his legal skills, as if they'd had the wind knocked out of them and couldn't speak. Defendants felt exposed, naked, and vulnerable on the stand against him. The people he put away for life felt that he had stolen their lives and killed them.

---

[1] Noumenon—that which is conceivable to the mind but not perceptible to the senses, such as God or the soul.

We found everything his mother had done to him, in his own form. Although he'd never owned it before, and had never brought those two sides together, he saw how he was just like her.

He was relatively wealthy and successful, a survivor who feared no one. He'd already been through the worst, and his indomitable will to live literally blazed from his eyes. When he finally saw the gifts his mother had given him—his will, strength, determination, and his whole career of protecting society from aggressors—he opened his heart to his mother. It was astonishing how much love he felt for the woman who had tried to kill him so many times. He saw that it was all love—that she wasn't going to be there, so she had perfectly prepared him to take care of himself, an extreme version of "A Boy Named Sue," the character in the song by Shel Silverstein and Johnny Cash.

The instant this man saw the blessings that came from his extraordinary experiences, and that the benefits perfectly balanced the difficulties, his heart spontaneously opened up to his mother. His face lost ten years and seemed to radiate light. The deep but repressed love he had always had for her came flooding out. That experience changed his life. He stopped trying to seek revenge upon her by proxy, and changed his career, going into preventive law to help people before they got into the justice system and were imprisoned. He stopped judging his mother so deeply and began to release his many judgments of himself and others.

> *"In a dark time, the eye begins to see."*
> — Theodore Roethke

You are a full-quantum being, but in your mind, you can be fooled and deny or disown half of yourself. When you imagine that you have more positives than negatives, you disown half of your experience, and the negativity becomes your disowned part. Ironically, whatever you disown in yourself you attract *into* your life in one form or another. You marry your disowned parts, become business partners with them, and attract them as clients and friends. Whatever you don't want to see or appreciate in yourself, you keep attracting into your life until you learn to love it. You can't escape your full quantum.

When you open your heart by acknowledging the magnificent design of the universe that you've been given, with *no mistakes,* just positive and negative homing devices to guide you, you start to be grateful. Gratitude is the key that opens the gateway of the heart and allows the unified field theory of love to fill your life. Gratitude makes you *present* with whatever you're doing. You are not here to run from away from sadness to happiness, because fulfillment is not possible when you deny half of your existence. Either side alone is only half-fillment. Something grand and far beyond either of those fleeting emotional states is available to you. This book is not about the myth of happiness; it's about the truth of balanced perception that brings you back to love.

Pain and Pleasure

We all feel both pain and pleasure. Anytime you think you're feeling more pleasure than pain, you're living an illusion; you're repressing something and you don't even know it. Or whenever you think, *I'm having more pain than pleasure, I'm suffering right now,* that's also an illusion.

I've done this exercise thousands of times: I can take people who think they're depressed and ask them a series of questions, and they can take themselves out of depression and right into love. I can also take people who think they're happy and ask *them* a series of questions to take them out of happiness and into love. Both emotions are just illusions, lopsided perceptions. They are masks of tragedy and comedy that veil our true nature. The moment you balance your mind, your perceptions of pain and pleasure disappear.

Let's say you were doing some job around the house and you smashed your thumb with a hammer. Just as you began cursing and leaping around the room, the doorbell rang. If the person at the door had come to congratulate you on just winning $50 million in the lottery, you probably would notice little or no sensation of pain in your thumb. When pain and pleasure are perfectly balanced, both disappear.

When I was president of the Cancer Prevention and Control Association in Houston, Texas, I worked with many people who had what was called "severe intractable pain." Some were living on significantly high doses of medication. In an amazingly short time, I was able to take these people successfully through a mind exercise where they played with their perceptions and associated a series of pleasures with their pain. In almost every case, their unbearable pain diminished or simply vanished.

They'd ask, "Where did it go? This doesn't make sense, but I can't feel any pain at all. You didn't give me an injection or anything; all we did was talk. What's going on here?"

The funny thing is that pain and pleasure remain perfectly balanced at every moment, but you selectively attend to one side or the other and feel pleasure or pain accordingly. There is both pain and pleasure in youth and age, poverty and wealth, solitude and multitude, illness and wellness. There is happiness in hovels and misery in mansions, and vice versa. This may be completely contrary to popular belief, but nothing changes between any of those two polarities except the *forms* of pain and pleasure; in terms of quantity and quality, they are perfectly conserved.

You have the capacity at any given moment to realize this pleasure-pain partnership and bring your mind into balance. Doing so will release the love and light that lie dormant within you. It's hard to believe that something so seemingly simple could be the source of such extraordinary power. It's hidden, but so is electricity until you flick the switch and make the connection.

Love is simply a state of nonseparation, where you perceive no division between yourself and some aspect of the world. In that wholeness and oneness, you experience what the ancient Hindu philosophers described as the highest state of consciousness, where whatever you see is you—*Tat Tvam Asi,* "That Thou Art." That's what sets you above the ordinary and makes you *extraordinary.* To the degree you tap in to that state, your dreams are in your hands. You have access to an infinitude of possibility because you're now tuning in to your infinite potential through the balance of love.

In my profession, I don't just speak to audiences, I also work clinically with people, one on one. And in my experience with thousands upon thousands of people, I've seen that down inside the soul and the human heart of the individual is a core of radiant love. I have not met *one* parent who, deep down inside beyond the facade and emotional shell, didn't have an unbelievable amount of love for his or her children. No parents are without love for their children, and no children are without love for their parents.

That *is* the unified field theory, the unified force that immortalizes people. When you can tap in to that source, whatever you dream is yours. In that state, you know why you're here, you're filled with certainty, and your mind becomes clear and focused. When you feel worthy of having your dreams, they appear. Your innermost dominant thought becomes your outermost tangible reality. Whatever you think about—and thank about—you bring about.

You have the power to create what you imagine, in direct proportion to how much love and gratitude you have in life, because your self-worth allows you to magnetize and attract those things into your life and make your visions real. When you know that you are loved no matter what, you have great power.

Turning Lead into Gold

We each have a unique destiny, and the power to create it, but charged emotions often cloud our vision and cause us to lose sight of our dreams.

I once had the opportunity to work with a 13-year-old girl in California who dreamed of earning an Olympic gold medal. Since the age of four, she had been devoted to gymnastics; working an average of seven to eight hours a day, five and sometimes seven days a week. The gold medal was almost all she'd ever dreamed of. Her mother saw the dream and did everything she could to earn the money and whatever else it took to make the dream come true.

I was called in because her Russian coach, who was rough, tough, and extremely disciplined, was challenging the young gymnast to the point of being overwhelmed. He was harder on her than anyone else, and his brute-force tactics and criticism were just too much. She wasn't eating or sleeping properly, and she was losing her vitality. She simply couldn't handle the pressure. She kept missing one of her vaults because she was so distracted and afraid that she'd blow it and that the coach would ridicule her.

I sat down with this girl and went through every single detail of the vault until she could see it exactly the way she wanted to do it. I took her, in frame-by-frame slow motion, through every part of her run, jump, twist, and landing until she could visualize every element perfectly. We choreographed it backward and forward until she could do it flawlessly in her mind. The next time she got up, she did the vault perfectly. Until then, she hadn't been able to "see" it. Her emotions about her coach had impeded her innate skill.

Next, I went to the gym to meet with the coach, and he was really tough. Every time this girl or anybody else made the tiniest error, he made them climb a 40-foot rope ten times without using their legs. Ten times! That means if they made three errors in the first hour of practice, they had to climb the rope 30 times. This man was a former gold medalist himself, a very strong and powerfully built man who spoke English, and I went up and chatted with him.

I said, "Your tactics . . . I notice some of the girls are dropping out, some are feeling pretty confronted, and their health is suffering. They're not eating, they're frightened," and so on.

He said something that shifted my perspective and really helped me. In his intense, broken English, he said, "I come from Russia; America hired me to come here. I come for gold; I am here to make gold. They cannot make mistakes. If they go one millimeter over, ten years of their lives is thrown away. It has to be *perfect* for the gold. They will hate me, they will think I am terrible and scream at me and not want to look at me, until the day they get their gold. Then I will be the first one they come to and hug. I am not here to be liked; I am here for gold! For America!"

I went back and shared his inspiration with the young girl. I took her through The Quantum Collapse Process to help her see the benefits of his challenging manner. So many people, including her mother, were supporting her with pleasure that the balancing challenge or pain had to come from somewhere, and it was from him. When she reframed her perspective on the value of his discipline and saw it as *love*, her performance became phenomenal. She realized that her coach's discipline was a sign that he loved her, saw her potential, and thought that she was capable of the gold. He was tougher on her than on anybody because he knew it would crush her to lose after all those years of work. If he allowed her to be anything less than perfect, that little margin of error would make the difference between silver, bronze, or no medal at all. Being nice could cost that young girl her life's dream.

With this new understanding, the girl's entire perspective changed, and she started working even beyond her normal practice sessions. She saw both sides of love and was able to turn the base metal of illusion into the gold of inspiration. When she felt the love, she had the power, she could see her dream clearly again, and she was that much closer to fulfillment. When you see both particle sides, pleasure and pain equally, the lightbulb turns on.

We often don't realize that it's the challenging people in our lives, working hand in hand with the supportive ones, who help us get where we're going in life. We need that balance of support and challenge, of positive and negative feedback, to grow and evolve. We have a lower, mortal nature that wants to have it all nice, sweet, supportive, and pleasurable, but in reality, we attract the other side to keep us balanced and on track. We're in the *illusion* that we want one-sidedness, but in our search for the monopole (a single positive or negative electrical charge), we find the balance of duality. The degree to which we appreciate both sides and embrace life is the degree to which we become enlightened.

The Perfection of Two Sides

A coin has two sides, heads and tails. I like to think of self-worth in terms of how many coins you accumulate in your life. If you allow yourself to embrace only the positive *heads* side, then the second somebody tries to give you a coin (an experience) that builds your self-worth, you say, "I don't want half of that." When you want only the positive and keep pushing away the negative, you can't get the coin. Most of us spend our lives trying to run from pain and seek pleasure, instead of embracing both in the pursuit of fulfilling our purpose.

Have you ever thought, *When I get this car, house, job, or relationship, life will be better?* Most people think that when they get something else, life will get better, but that kind of thinking only transforms the positives and negatives into new forms. I'm not saying you shouldn't seek, but if you think something will give you more positives than negatives, you're living with an illusion. When you get what you imagine you want, you'll find out that it comes with a catch or a twist that you didn't anticipate. You only get a new set of pains and pleasures.

If you run your life thinking that you'll have pleasure without pain, you're setting yourself up for the very pain you seek to avoid. When you don't see the perfection of where you are, you take the pure energy of inspiration and dissipate it in emotional reactions. You swing back and forth between "I'm happy, I'm sad. I'm happy, I'm sad." Or in a relationship, "I'm attracted, I'm repelled. I like you, I dislike you. I can't be *away* from you, I can't live *with* you."

As long as you're in your physical body, you're destined to have this duality, because you're an oscillating homing device and you're going *home*. You're zeroing in on your destiny, and during that process, you get elated and depressed, and then elated and depressed again. Maximal evolution occurs at the border between attraction and repulsion, pleasure and pain, order and chaos, like and dislike. Between the extremes lie the light, love, and true *power* to create the life you aspire to.

That's why I make the following statement, as shocking as it may seem at first: *All emotions are lies.* The truth is love, but emotions are half-truths, distortions, and lies. There is nothing but love, and all else is illusion. We go through life merely living instead of embracing it all. We oscillate between our positive and negative emotions because we don't love.

You don't have command over anything that you have emotions about; you only have command over the things you love. Love is a perfectly equilibrated, divinely ordained state of consciousness that's available to you 24 hours a day if you just balance your mind and don't let it go off on emotional illusions. I'm all for feelings of love, but just know that every expression and repression of emotion will run your life. Love is *not* an emotion; it *transcends* emotion. It is the synthesis of all polar-opposite emotions. Some say that love is blind, but it's not; it sees clearly. Emotions are blind because they see only one side. When you run your life by infatuations and resentments, you disempower yourself. You give your power away—not because of anything others do, but because of what *you* do.

The gift of this planet is that you're surrounded by love, because the definition of love is both sides of experience: praise and reprimand, support and challenge, being lifted up and put down simultaneously. That is divine will. Theology describes it as the right and left hand of the Creator coming down to make sure you're always in balance. When you see and honor this balance, your life is transformed; you're liberated.

All positive and negative particles in the universe come in complementary pairs; at every level of creation they come into existence simultaneously. Everything has two sides. Scientists have recently found that the bubonic plague, the Black Death that swept through Europe and killed one-third of the population in the 14th century, has bequeathed immunity to AIDS, the great plague of the 21st century. More than 10 percent of those of European descent carry an immunity to this modern virus. That same plague also destroyed the feudal system that perpetuated extreme poverty and stifled education and social evolution. From death comes new life.

There is a divine justice system, and you can't screw it up. Have you ever noticed that when somebody tries to praise you beyond your true worth, you'll put yourself down in front of them? And if someone tries to cut you down below your true worth, you'll lift yourself up to balance it? If you're judging yourself too harshly, the divine justice system will do whatever it takes to equilibrate you. No human justice system can approach the perfection of divine justice; it is beyond our full comprehension.

The Bars Are Ours

People often say to me in consultations, "You know, my life is a mess. Everything is all screwed up," but I have yet to meet anyone with a screwed-up life, just people who haven't learned to find the hidden balance in their lives. I once did a radio show in Los Angeles, and at the very end, a gentleman somehow called in from prison. He was crying on the phone, so choked up he could barely speak.

He said, "I've been in prison now for 11 years, for rape and murder, and you just gave me a new reason to live. You said that it's impossible to take something without also giving, because life maintains a balance. I've been punishing myself for 11 years over what I did, but I just realized that in this prison, I have become the counselor who saves lives. There are a lot of people here who want to commit suicide or shoot up drugs, and I'm the one who's talked them out of it. *I have saved lives.* Even I have a mission in this place, and I never found it until I listened to this radio show. I knew that I had taken life, but now I see how I've saved it. I also realize that if I wasn't here, I'd have killed myself with drugs by now, so prison actually saved my life, too."

When he realized that he'd gone through those events in his life for a significant purpose, to be in that prison and save lives, he could then say, "Now I have fulfillment. I appreciate my position in life. Thank you, God. Thank you for this radio show." At that moment, the murderer found the hidden balance to his actions and was free to live again. He truly changed his life.

I'm amazed by the number of people I meet every week who believe they will one day get to perfection, instead of acknowledging that they already *are* perfection. They live under the illusion that they weren't perfect in some situation, that if they had acted differently, they would have been. The duality is the perfection, and the combination of the two sides serves to put us right into our hearts.

The heart is more powerful than the intellect in this area. It knows the truth and waits patiently, while the mind slowly comes to an enlightened understanding. The rest of this book is devoted to waking your mind up to the perfection that already exists, so your heart can come forward and direct your life.

Exercise 1

If you're still judging yourself, beating yourself up for something you've done or not done, it's time to look deeply and see how it served you and others and get on with your life. It's impossible to harm someone without directly or indirectly helping them at exactly the same time, because everything is balanced, and everything ultimately serves physically or metaphysically. That's not an excuse, it's the truth, so it's wise to wake up and stop punishing yourself over any illusions.

If there's a fragment somewhere in your life that you think is too difficult to love, just know that that's an illusion. You *are* truly worthy of love. Say this affirmation: *"No matter what I have done or have not done, I am worthy of love."* When every single cell of your body gets it, so will you, and so will your world. When we love, we step into the full quantum state, we align ourselves with the forces of life, and the power of the whole *universe* is suddenly behind us.

Exercise 2

Every person, place, thing, idea, and event in your life has two sides, and when you see them clearly, you realize that everything is love and you can be grateful. I encourage you to take the time to do this exercise, even if you have to do it in little chunks and pieces.

1. Look back over your life and identify every single thing that you think was somehow negative—that is, not meaningful and purposeful and aligned with your destiny. For each item, ask yourself, "How was that an act of love? How did that serve me and others? How did that help me?" Don't stop until you can give thanks for each one.

2. Then ask, "How did that help me become what I am today? How did that person or event bless me and contribute to my mission?" You'll see that there was not one person or event that didn't equilibrate you and wake you up.

3. Imagine what it would be like if you could not see anything else around you but perfect equilibrium, and the more clearly you saw it, the more you saw the divine assistance. No matter what happened, you could turn it into guidance and fuel for your journey home or your destiny. When you know everything serves you, what can stop you?

Words of Wisdom and Power

- *I am made of light. What can harm me?*
- *I am worthy of having all of my dreams come true.*
- *How is this helping me fulfill my destiny?*
- *Love is all there is; everything else is illusion.*
- *No matter what I have done, or have not done,*
  I am worthy of love.

Chapter Three

Living Dreams

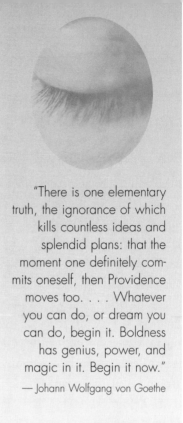

"There is one elementary truth, the ignorance of which kills countless ideas and splendid plans: that the moment one definitely commits oneself, then Providence moves too. . . . Whatever you can do, or dream you can do, begin it. Boldness has genius, power, and magic in it. Begin it now."

— Johann Wolfgang von Goethe

I believe that deep inside, at the core of our being and the essence of our existence, we all have a mission for life. We each have something of genius, something that calls to us. We live in an incredibly magnificent universe, and part of us knows this and calls to us with an infinite amount of energy to make sure we don't miss out on the gifts and opportunities that surround and fill us. Gratitude is the key to fulfillment. Gratitude and self-worth come hand in hand, and great worth comes from gratefully fulfilling our dreams. We all have a dream, a vision, and a purpose, and it takes only a moment of clarity and *presence* to bring it out. Everything that happens to us is crucial to the awakening of that essence, and one of the strongest directing forces is this dream we have inside.

My Great Mentor Appears

Before I was able to go to college and pursue my destiny of awakening human potential and discovering our relationship to light, a vital component needed to come to me. We all have great teachers who show up in our lives, great friends, loved ones, or guides who arrive at exactly the right time to give us the powerful lessons and experiences we need to fulfill our destiny. Mine appeared when I was 17 years old.

After leaving my first mentor in El Paso, I went to California, then on to Hawaii, where I lived my dream of surfing some of the biggest waves in the world. Once again, life showed me its balance when I contracted strychnine poisoning and nearly died. I remember walking outside a grocery store one day, feeling dizzy, and then blacking out. About four days later, I woke up in my tent hidden away in the Hawaiian jungle. I was covered with vomit, urine, and feces, completely dehydrated and virtually on my deathbed.

A lady who lived in the jungle nearby happened to be passing along a path by my tent and heard me groaning. After taking a quick look at me, she ran to get some fresh passion fruit juice, orange juice, and vitamin C, and she poured them down my throat. I wouldn't be here today if not for this woman. She appeared to help me at the very moment of my greatest helplessness, staying with me for four days to clean me up and care for me.

On the fourth day, she helped me walk to a little nearby health-food store, and as we walked out, I saw a flyer on the door. It said "Yoga Class—Special guest speaker: Paul Bragg. Sunset Recreation Hall, Waimea Bay."

Something inside me told me to go. I wanted to gain control over my weakened and spasmodic body, and I had heard that yoga could help integrate body and mind, but more than all those logical reasons, that little flyer was somehow calling me.

I walked into a room with about 35 people, all of whom were sitting on towels. Standing in front of them was a 93-year-old gentleman who had perfect vision and all his hair and teeth. He was an absolutely alive, vibrant, present individual, such as I'd never met before.

He started to lecture on what he called "universal laws." He said we're only as old as our spines, and if our spines are rigid, so are our bodies and minds, and if we lose our visions and inspirations, we decay and die. In his 45-minute talk, he spoke about things I had never heard or imagined before, and he *inspired* me.

At the end, he said, "All right, you young people, tonight we're going to decide your *destiny*. We're going to find out what you're going to do for the rest of your life—we're going to determine your life's purpose. I'm going to give you ten minutes to reflect, and think about what you want to dedicate your life to, then I'm going to take you through an experience, and it's going to come true."

When you're 17 years old and someone tells you that *exactly* what you decide right now will happen in your life, it's a pretty spooky experience. But his certainty was far greater than my doubt (and whoever has the most certainty rules), so I sat there on the floor and reflected on what I truly wanted to do with my life.

Sitting there, I suddenly flashed back to Mrs. McLaughlin, my first-grade teacher, saying, "I'm afraid your son will never read, write, or communicate. He'll never amount to anything." I then flashed to the old bum in El Paso with his emphasis on love and wisdom. Next I saw myself lying in my tent, nearly dead, and finally I flashed back to the room, looked up at Paul Bragg, and said to myself inwardly, "I know what I want to do; I know *exactly* what I want to do. I want to dedicate the rest of my life to the study of universal laws, as they relate to mind, body, and spirit, particularly in relation to healing. I want to travel the world and share that with people."

In that moment, I *knew*. I can't describe exactly how that felt, but it was an incredible revelation. Each of us has some special moment when we know what we're here to do. Sometimes we filter it out with doubt, fear, and guilt, but our spirits and hearts know, and they wake us up in momentary glimpses and call us to action.

In my life, that was my time.

Then Paul Bragg said, "All right, now that you know, we're going to do a special guided-imagery meditation." He had a mandala,[1] and he came to each of us in turn and said, "Open your eyes. Look at the mandala. Close your eyes. Open your eyes. Look at the mandala. Close your eyes."

He guided us through an incredible experience. During the exercise, I imagined myself walking through an arched stone tunnel with light at the end. I came to a balcony overlooking a huge square where 40 feet below stood what seemed to be a million people. I began to speak, sharing a message on universal laws and spiritual healing.

That virtual picture was so vivid that I couldn't distinguish it from reality. I sat there crying tears of inspiration for 15 minutes, overwhelmed by such a revelation about my destiny. In that moment, I knew from the depth of my heart what I would love to do.

In your heart, you, too, know what you would love to do, even though there may be a part of you that doesn't think you can do it. (Or, if you think you don't know, you will by the end of this book.) Never lose the dream, because it *is* your love and your wisdom. Nothing can take it away from you.

I came out of the meditation, and Paul Bragg said, "Well, you young folks, I really appreciate your having me here. By the way, every morning I have a little gathering of my students in the barracks at the center of the island. If you'd like to join us, please come. Gather! We'll get some exercise, some fresh water and fruit, and have a little class."

The next morning, I hitchhiked to the center of the island and met him at the barracks, where about 20 students had gathered. They

---

[1] Mandala—a balanced and harmonious symbol, drawing, or image of universal wholeness.

ranged from 50 to 80 years old, and I was the only teenager.

After some calisthenics, we ran three to four miles. I could barely keep up. We came back and stretched, drank some distilled water, and ate some fruit, then he lectured again on universal laws.

Every day for the next three weeks, I hitchhiked to the barracks and learned everything I could about universal laws. I was in the presence of a masterful human being, a man with a global vision, and it was a crucial time in my life. It was like I was a fresh floppy disk that this great computer was downloading onto.

At the end of the three weeks, Paul said, "Well, that'll be all folks. I'm heading back to California. I really appreciate your being with me, and I hope to see you in the future. Love you all. See you soon."

My heart sank, because all of a sudden my mentor was disappearing. Until that moment, I had never had the courage to speak to him, but I spoke up then. I waited until everyone else had left, and I said, "Uh, Mr. Bragg?"

"Yes, young man?"

"Sir, I'm John Demartini, and I was at your class about three weeks ago."

"Yes, I remember you. How can I help you?"

"Well, sir, you said that whatever we decided upon that night for our life was going to happen. But you see, sir, I don't know how I can do that. It seems a little overwhelming to me. I don't know how I can get my dream because I was told I would never read, write, or communicate, and I've never read a complete book in my life. I don't know *how* to read very well, and I have a very limited vocabulary."

"Son, here's how you solve that. I want you to say something to yourself, and I want you to say this every single day for the rest of your life and never miss a day. I want you to commit to this."

"What's that, sir?"

"I want you to say to yourself, 'I am a genius, and I apply my wisdom.' Say it, young man."

"I'mageniusandIapplymywisdom?"

"No, no, no, no, son. No. I don't mean say it, I mean *say* it. It has to be said from deep inside."

"Uh, I'm a genius, and I apply my wisdom?"

"No, son, say it again."

"I'mageniusandI—"

"*No,* son! You have to say this until you mean it. It's got to come from the depths of your being. And you have to say it every single day and never miss a day, until *every single cell* in your body gets it. When every single cell in your body gets it, so will this world. So you say it every single day."

He made me say it over and over and over and over and over, until my eyes closed and I became present with that statement. When I became present, I could see my vision again. I was standing out on that balcony. I brought those words and that vision together, and I repeated them and got a feeling of inspiration. I somehow felt that this was going to change my life. I didn't know how, but his certainty was greater than my doubt, and, as I've said before, whoever has the most certainty rules. Bragg ruled my state of consciousness by his *certainty*, his *presence*, his *love* for the destiny that I was to unfold, and his *gratitude* for the laws of the universe that made it possible.

"I'm a genius, and I apply my wisdom. I'm a *genius*, and I apply my wisdom." I thanked him and felt like I had been given a gift. I didn't understand the significance of it to the extent that I do today, but I knew I'd been given something.

I remember hitchhiking back to my tent, standing on the road and thinking to myself, *I'm a genius, and I . . . I apply my wisdom. I'm a genius, and I apply my wisdom."* After about 15 cars went by, I started to doubt it and thought, *Yeah, well, why is a genius hitchhiking?* But I finally got a ride back to the campsite, still affirming to myself, *I'm a genius, and I apply my wisdom. I'm a genius, and I apply my wisdom.*

When I got to my tent, three of my buddies were there, so I lifted the flap and said, "Hey, guys, guess what? I'm a *genius*, and I apply my *wisdom*!" and they all went, "All rrriiight! John's a genius! Woo! Woo! Woo! Woooo!"

At that moment, I realized I wasn't going to share my dreams with any but a select group of people. There's power in maintaining your vision, inspiration, and purpose within, and in wisely choosing the people with whom you share it.

Dreams Come True

After that vision and experience, I left Hawaii and went back home to Richmond. I now had something important to do with my life, and there wasn't a moment to waste. I devoted myself to learning how to read and study, took a high school equivalency test and some college entrance exams, and just a few months later, entered Wharton Junior College in Wharton, Texas. Because I had believed for so long that I could never do anything academic, I took the opportunity seriously and studied very hard.

I was in the library one day almost two years later, preparing for a calculus test, when one of my classmates came up to me and said, "John, can I study with you?"

I said, "Sure, come on."

Then someone else asked, "Hey, John! Can I study with you, too?"

"Yeah. Yeah, sure you can!"

A whole bunch of students joined me, forming three concentric circles around the table and asking me questions. I was tutoring them in calculus. Me! I heard one guy whisper, "That John, he's a genius. He's a friggin' *genius*."

When I heard him say that, I started to have a tear of inspiration. I couldn't *help* it, because my impossible dream had started to come true. I remembered what Paul Bragg had said: "If you say this one statement to yourself, if you make a commitment to say it every single day and never miss a day in your life, sooner or later every cell in your body, every fragment of your consciousness, will start to harmonize and be with you. The *moment* you start to integrate it, you will notice that the people around you will start to recognize your genius."

"The will to be oneself is heroism."
— José Ortega y Gasset

After that day in the library, I started making some new affirmations because I realized that what I said to myself made a huge difference. I wrote down enough affirmations to fill a day with nonstop internal conversation. I wrote only those statements that inspired me and aligned with my vision. These later proved to have a major impact on my life.

When I was very young, an elderly lady named Mrs. Grubbs lived next door to us. One day, she saw me pulling weeds in the yard to earn a quarter from my parents. She leaned across the fence and said, "John, if you keep focusing on those weeds and don't plant flowers in your garden, you're going to be pulling weeds forever. You must learn to plant, and focus on the flowers."

I realized that my mind was now a garden, and it was my job— *no one else's*—to plant my dreams—my statements, ideas, and visual images of how I wanted my life to be. I made a disciplined decision to focus on my dreams *no matter what*. I became a top student and eventually entered the health profession and my chosen career, but it took me a long time before I figured out what true genius is: *A genius is one who sees the guiding light of their soul, listens to the internal message, and obeys.*

The Price of Dreams

To be a genius, you must be willing to do whatever it takes to achieve your dreams, but there's always a price. There are three forces that motivate people. The first two are avoiding pain and seeking pleasure; these are fueled by desperation. The third, inspiration, transcends the others. Being motivated by desperation won't guarantee you purposeful fulfillment, and when things get challenging, you'll more than likely give up. But inspiration knows the costs and challenges, as well as the rewards and benefits, and does it anyway.

When you're inspired, you embrace both pain and pleasure in the pursuit of your purpose. Professional football players know that they're going to spend the next 40 years living with the effects of broken knees and tissue damage. Astronauts know that going into space might bring muscle atrophy, bone-density loss, brain damage, and even death. I know that as I travel 300 days a year to speak around the world, I get three times the amount of radiation permitted for pilots, I'm away from my family, I live in hotels, and . . . that's just the way it is.

I've never met a successful person who didn't have trials and tribulations and positive and negative feedback along the way. Wisdom is looking back at your life and realizing that every single event, person, place, and idea was part of the perfected experience you needed to build your dream. Not *one* was a mistake. Mrs. McLaughlin, the cowboys, the bum on the street, the lady at my tent, Paul Bragg—even the people who gave me rides when I was hitch-hiking—were all part of a magnificent design. The same principle applies to you and the life of every human being: Everything serves, and the bigger the crisis, the larger the blessing.

If you look at the great leaders of the world, they were supreme-ly focused on what they did. If you want to excel at something, then let no day go by without dedicating your life 100 percent to making it happen. Time is precious.

As a well-known real estate developer in New York City became increasingly successful, more and more people wanted to do business with him. They'd make a one-hour appointment and spend the first quarter-hour establishing rapport; the next quarter talking about themselves, their company, or his company; finally get down to business for the third 15 minutes; then finish by repeating it all over again. He realized he was getting through only a few proposals a day, and much of his time was spent on things of little or no value to him, so he came up with a fantastic strategy to get to his priorities. He bought a 15-minute hourglass, and when someone walked into his office, he'd turn it over and say, "You've got 15 minutes to make your pitch. Go!" He made them get real, get clear, and get present. If they weren't focused enough to sell him in that time, he gave them a decision right away. His business and energy went *way* up as a result.

One of my wife's friends is a successful Australian businessman. She once asked him, "What is the key to success?" and he replied, "Try *really* working eight hours a day. I mean, be *present* eight hours a day."

What would happen if you were fully present eight hours a day? What if you knew exactly what you wanted and allowed nothing to distract you from your focus and your inspiration? Successful people focus their attention on the gold medal, the Academy Award, the absolute mastery of their chosen field. To achieve their dreams, they practice between performances, and they develop the power of *sustained attention.*

Sustained attention demands clear consciousness, but consciousness can be clouded by fear. Many years ago, I had a major fear of public speaking. It was a daunting challenge for me to face, but conquering this fear changed my life.

In my very first class in professional school, the professor said, "You're all going to give a talk. You must select from one of the given topics, choose a date, and give your presentation before the class."

My talk was about six weeks away, and I chose to speak on "Referred Pain: The Impact of Pain and Pleasure on the Human Psyche." Even the subject was part of life's perfection and my destiny; today I work with people who assume that there is pain without pleasure in this universe, which is both a myth and a mystery.

I hadn't spoken in public before, and from the moment I got the assignment, I started having anxiety. It began with heart palpitations on the first day, and more symptoms developed with every day that passed. The day before my speech, I had diarrhea, a sore throat, memory loss, dizziness, itchy eyes, bumps on my tongue, and stomach cramps. The next morning, I got to class knowing that I'd have to speak. As the girl sitting in front of me got up to give her talk, she grabbed my hand and said, "Wish me luck," but while she spoke, all I could think was, *Oh my God! It's my time!*

Sitting there awaiting my turn, I forgot the title of my talk, I forgot my topic, I forgot my *name*. I forgot everything—I didn't know who I was! Finally, she finished, and the professor called . . . the person behind me. He skipped right over me, and to this day, I have never given that talk. I was the only person in class who didn't speak.

That night I went home and cried, not from sorrow that I didn't get to talk, but sorrow that I had let six weeks of my life go by in paralyzing anxiety over something that never even occurred. Have you ever had perceived misery and anxiety over something that turned out to be nothing? At that moment, I made a commitment. I said to myself, "I will do whatever it takes, travel whatever distance, and pay whatever price, to *master* this thing called speaking." The next day I signed up for every council in the school. I took on every opportunity to speak because I was determined to master it.

I faced my fears and set out to master public speaking, and years later I was asked to speak in Las Vegas before 8,000 people, where I got to meet author and lecturer Wayne Dyer. While he was getting ready for a photo session, I quickly said, "I would like to become an international professional speaker. Can you give me some advice and direction?"

Dyer is a very tall man, and he looked down at me and said quietly, "Just start telling people that you're an international professional speaker." The expression on my face was like, "Uh-uh, and what else?" so he repeated, "Just start telling people that." He kept it really simple.

I said, "Oka-a-a-y, I'm an international professional speaker."

That one idea changed what I said to myself and to others, and whenever anybody asked me what I did, I said, "I'm an international professional speaker." Only a few weeks later, I was asked to speak in Canada, to give a paid speech internationally, and I thought, *My God, it works!*

The masses wait to see it to believe it, but the master believes it and *then* sees it. The master affirms and believes it ahead of time. We create our lives with our thoughts, every minute of the day. I made a commitment to myself that one day I was going to speak on a program with Wayne Dyer, and last year I gave three presentations back-to-back with him. I made the commitment, and it happened. I wanted to set foot on every major country on Earth and be paid to do it, and now new countries constantly open up to me. This year it was Austria, Spain, and some in South America, and I really believe it's because I was clear about what I wanted. I took the time to decide exactly how I'd love my life, visualized as many details as I could imagine, wrote them all down, and then took action. Write it down! Things that aren't put down on paper get left in the mind, and a short pencil is better than a long memory when it comes to your dreams.

The Dream Is in the Detail

Are you clear about what you would love? Do you know exactly how you would love it? Do you see it in so much detail that when you close your eyes you can't see anything *but* your life the way you would love it? What would happen if you had no distractions or obstacles in your mind and couldn't imagine anything else? If you kept refining your dream until it was all you could see? When you can't imagine it any other way, that's the way it happens . . . and is often when it begins to happen.

> *"You are what your deep, driving desire is.*
> *As your desire is, so is your will.*
> *As your will is, so is your deed.*
> *As your deed is, so is your destiny."*
> — The Upanishads

A gentleman who'd been a guest on *Oprah* came into my office some years ago and asked me, "How did you get your seminars happening around the world?"

I said, "Well, it's my vision," and I pulled out my dream book to show him my detailed visual master plan.

He said, "No, no, no, I want to see your brochures. I want to know how you marketed it."

"I don't have any brochures," I responded.

"But what was your marketing strategy?"

"I have a clear vision, and whenever and wherever I speak, I stay fully present and inspired."

"Yeah, I know, but what do you mail out to people? How do you reach them?"

He was stuck on the idea that the power was in a brochure or some slick marketing piece. I said, "You keep projecting artificial limits onto a successful strategy for building dreams. What I'm telling you is that if you truly become crystal clear on how you would love your life, to such a degree that you can't see anything *but* that, it's almost impossible for you not to get it." Absolute clarity adds vitality and enthusiasm to your actions.

I believe that this principle is worth repeating: If you get absolutely crystal clear on exactly what you would love, and you can't see anything *but* that, it's almost impossible for you not to get it. If you can say, "I am worth it, I deserve to have my dreams, I deserve to take the time to focus on the infinite details to create them, I have a human will, and I'll align it with divine will and allow it to fill me and inspire me to write out each dream in a specific fashion," and then you do it . . . then it's yours.

Miss Houston

I had the opportunity to work with a beautiful and talented young lady in Texas who wanted to win the Miss Houston beauty pageant— it was her dream; it inspired her. She was a singer, she did pantomime and ventriloquism and other performance arts, and she was just beginning to expand her beauty career.

When she sat down with me, she said, "Dr. Demartini, I'd like to speak with you about my dream of becoming Miss Houston."

I asked her, "What do you see?"

"I see myself being Miss Houston."

"Yes, but what *exactly* do you see? How do you see it?"

We found that the picture in her mind was a bit fragmented, and the holes in her vision matched the challenging obstacles she was attracting. As I worked with this aspiring young lady, I had her imagine how she would walk, how she'd carry the bouquet, how every part of her face and body would look, how the audience and the stage and the hall would look—everything.

She thought about what she'd say in her speech, which questions they'd ask and how she'd respond, what she would sing, what she would wear, and how she'd present herself. We went through it in ever finer detail, clarifying everything she could see on stage, and we hit it from every angle until she couldn't see anything *but* winning Miss Houston. She started to tear up with inspiration because she was *there*. At that moment, she had certainty. She won Miss Houston because she couldn't see anything else.

How much energy do *you* spend on obstacles and distractions because you haven't taken the time to define your mission and your dreams? What would happen if you honored and disciplined yourself to define your destiny? What could you create? The universe is doing everything it can to wake you up and make sure you get your dreams. If you reframe your mind so that no matter what happens, no matter whom you meet, no matter what the situation or challenge or obstacle, you experience it as helping you to fulfill your dream, how can you fail?

You won't rise above and beyond anything you're charged and emotional about, so the best way to do what you love is to love what you're doing right now. State your dream clearly, and then ask yourself how what you're doing right now is preparing you for your dreams. When you love and are grateful for what *is,* you get the power to turn it into what you love.

If you know that no matter what happens, your life is serving your dreams, then nothing can stop you. The minute you truly commit to your dream, watch the universe immediately bring you the sustenance *and* the challenges necessary to fulfill it. Positive or negative, supportive or challenging, peaceful or warlike, cooperative or competitive, pleasurable or painful—no matter *what* happens, if you can see how it's serving you, how can you not succeed?

Secrets of an Inspired Life

Living an inspired life requires mastering some skills, one of which is the ability to ask yourself inspirational, meaningful questions. The quality of your life is determined by the quality of the questions you ask. If you say to yourself, *I'd like to do that, but how can I when I don't have the money?* you create a mind-set that assumes you can't and stops without even trying. If, instead, you ask yourself, *How can I do what I love and be magnificently paid for it?* and don't stop looking until you find the answer, you'll get an entirely different outcome and life. Reframing the questions you ask yourself offers tremendous power.

The second secret to an inspired life is the Law of Greatest Efficiency. This law tells us that anyone or anything that doesn't fulfill its purpose automatically decays. The matter that's utilized in this universe gets dissipated and redistributed to those who are willing to fulfill their divine design. That which becomes extinct gives rise to that which is ever greater, so it's vital to be clear about your purpose. That's why I say that there's nothing wrong with retirement as long as it doesn't get in the way of your work, because the second you stop growing, you automatically undergo entropy. But even when you're not inspired and consciously following your mission, you still play a part in the divine order. There's nothing wrong if you feel like you're off purpose. Just know that your resources, energy, and life will be given to somebody else who is inspired and feeling purposeful.

Here's one final secret: The purpose of The Breakthrough Experience, and probably why you were drawn to it, is to offer you a more efficient way to listen to your own heart and soul, the inner wisdom that is infinitely greater than any external teaching. It is the *true* teacher, and when you have access to it, you begin to pay more attention to its wise guidance. When you glimpse an understanding of the universal laws and divine order, when you awaken your sense of gratitude for the marvelous gift of life, you become inspired to live the dream you were created to fulfill.

Exercise

Create the life you love:

1. Every day, sit for a moment in silent meditation and concentrate on exactly what you would love to create in your life. Imagine every detail you can, and then even more. See your life exactly the way you would love it to be. Let your imagination be real enough to come true, yet ideal enough to inspire and stretch you.

2. Write down all that you can imagine, and begin formulating your goals. Writing down your dreams helps them come true, so include all the details.

3. Every day, take at least one action step toward making your goals come true. What you move toward moves toward you.

4. Keep records of every synchronous, goal-aligned event that occurs; they fill your life when you stop to acknowledge them. Write down all the events that come true each day that demonstrate that you're moving in the direction of your dreams.

5. Keep refining your goals, becoming clearer with each passing day about what you would love to create.

6. As you begin to fulfill these goals, be sure to add new ones, all revolving around your chief aim or purpose in life.

7. Maintain an achievement and blessing journal. Be thankful for every supportive and challenging event that occurs to give you feedback and fulfillment on the road to your dreams.

(Also, you might want to read my book *Count Your Blessings— The Healing Power of Gratitude and Love,* for other creative insights about goals and purpose.)

Words of Wisdom and Power

- *I see my dreams with crystal clarity.*
- *I am worthy of having my dreams come true.*
- *The pain of regret outweighs the pain of discipline.*
- *A genius listens to the guidance of the soul, and obeys.*
- *I am a genius, and I apply my wisdom.*
- *I do what I love, and I love what I do.*

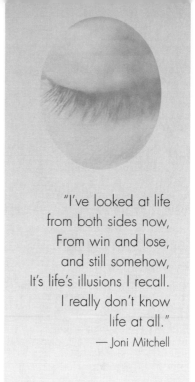

Chapter Four

Both Sides Now

"I've looked at life
from both sides now,
From win and lose,
and still somehow,
It's life's illusions I recall.
I really don't know
life at all."
— Joni Mitchell

The last chapter explored the power and importance of living your dreams. A vital element in living those dreams is the ability to remain centered and balanced, no matter what happens. In the center are the light, the spirit, the power, and the certainty that allow you to stay on your path, and they make up your true nature. You might very well ask, "If we're all light, then why are we so often confused, and how did we forget our enlightened nature?" The answer is lopsided sensory perceptions.

As long as you have lopsided perceptions instead of a divinely balanced mind, you won't be able to run your life from your heart. Everyone has the capacity to do what they love, love what they do, and live an inspired life, but lopsided perceptions create an emotion that distracts and runs you. Until you bring yourself back into perceptual balance, you fragment yourself into self-righteous and "self-wrongeous" personas, which psychologists often call your owned and disowned parts.

Personas are the masks that conceal your true nature. How are personas formed? Every time you lie about the universe, you simultaneously create two of them—the self-righteous and the self-wrongeous mask. If you have 1,000 lies about divine order and balance, you have 2,000 personas, and all those aspects of yourself compete for your consciousness, lower your potential, and keep you from remembering who you really are.

When you think that you're more positive than negative, you get self-righteous and build yourself up, and when you see more negatives than positives, you get self-wrongeous and beat yourself down. When you're up, you feel elated and act self-righteously and superior toward other people; and when you're down, you feel depressed and act self-wrongeously and inferior.

Let's say you come home from school one day and see your parents arguing. Your dad gets angry and shouts and your mother cries, and you automatically assume he's bad and she's good. You don't know what the argument is about or how his anger may be serving her, but you label one good and the other bad and separate yourself into two personas that hold those beliefs.

Because of something called *compound association,* it doesn't stop there. A week or a month later, you may be playing under a friend's house and hear his father speaking loudly. Your mind instantly associates that moment with the time your father shouted at your mother, and it unconsciously connects darkness and the smell of mold under the house to badness. Maybe your friend's father has no hair, so you also make a connection that bald men are not to be trusted. Later still, you see a bald man driving a big car, so big cars get linked in, too.

Eventually, almost everything is split into good and bad. Men, mold, cars, and the other associations are really neutral, neither good nor bad, but you can't see this because your personas cause you to over- and underreact to associated events in your life.

Have you ever found yourself in some situation of conflict, and thought, *I can't believe I'm saying this?* That's a persona temporarily taking over in a moment of stress. Every time some voice inside says, "Who do you think you are? You can't do that. You don't belong here," just know that one of your personas is frightened by your dreams because it doesn't have the power to fulfill them, but the whole integrated you does.

Who Do You Think You Are?

Years ago, when The Breakthrough Experience was being conceived, I was asked to do an infomercial. The studio set was arranged, a host introduced me, and I came out onto the stage. All of a sudden, the electrical systems blew and there was no audio or video. I was in front of an audience who didn't know me and wasn't highly interested in being there. When I said, "Good evening!" they just stared in dead silence.

"Any questions on what I've covered so far?" I was trying to get them to laugh, but a European lady with hair piled two feet high and gold safety chains dangling from her glasses said, "Young man, *I* have a question for you. Who *are* you? And who do you think you are? What gives you the right to stand up there and imagine you have something to tell us?"

My self-righteous side was saying in a deep and reasonable voice, "Well, I'm a doctor of chiropractic, and these are my degrees, and this is my background . . . ," while my other side was saying in a high-pitched, squeaky voice, "I must be an idiot. What the heck *am* I doing here?"

All of a sudden, out of those two came this: "I am a person on a quest to study universal laws as they relate to mind, body, and spirit, particularly in relation to health. I've dedicated my life to it, and I've learned on that journey that whatever I say to you is what I'm working on in myself. I'm honored to have someone like you here so I can learn and grow."

She pushed her glasses up higher on her nose and said with a nod, "Young man, please proceed. You have my attention." From that point on, everybody was focused, the microphones came back on, and we continued.

I could have been self-righteous or self-wrongeous, but by becoming integrated, I became present and had a real effect on the people. True and balanced love cannot be rejected; only false expectations and exaggerated or minimized expectations can. False expectations are *designed* to be rejected, because the universe wants us to love.

The self-righteous persona takes credit for everything you think goes right, the self-wrongeous persona takes the blame for everything you think goes wrong, and both block your true nature. When you reunite the two personas/particles of yourself, you regain your true nature as light. When you stop taking credit and blame, you have the potential to become present, and in that state of presence, you're capable of what most people call *miracles*.

The Healing Power of Presence

I had a powerful experience relating to the miraculous healing power of presence about 20 years ago when a young boy who had been in a coma for three years was brought to my chiropractic office. He had been to 13 different hospitals and doctors, but no one had noticed that his skull was jammed down on his spinal cord and was cutting off all higher brain function from his body. They simply diagnosed his condition as brain-damaged encephalitis and said they couldn't help.

I took the boy on as a clinical challenge to see if I could assist him. His x-rays showed me this jamming of his brain and spinal cord, and I wondered, *What would happen if I lifted his skull and decompressed his brain and spinal cord?* Within me was also the thought, *He could die. Can I handle him dying in my hands?* I shook with fear at the thought of losing my new career if I adjusted him and he died.

I told his parents, "I don't know if I can help your son." His mother, a little Indian-Mexican woman, looked up at me with her deep, shining eyes and said, "If he dies, he dies. If he lives, we rejoice. But Dr. Demartini, we have nowhere else to go."

When she said that, my fear disappeared, my personas were integrated, and I went into a state where I wasn't taking credit or blame. I was willing to have him die in my hands and embrace it. I'd never had that experience in my life.

In my mind, the mother had given me a gift. In that moment, I was completely centered. I went to the boy and put my hand under his skull. I *saw* the skull and imagined the x-ray, and suddenly I felt a power like a freight train come through me. With the assistance of this tremendous power, I lifted the boy's skull off his jammed spine, and he suddenly came out of his coma. As he extended his once rigid and unmoving limbs, his entire family—mother, father, and six other children—fell to their knees and began to pray.

I went into another room and sat across the table from another doctor who had witnessed the event. We looked at each other and couldn't speak; we simply sat there in tears, knowing we had just seen the inborn power that brings life reawaken the boy's body. For the first time, I had seen a chiropractic adjustment fulfill its true potential, and it was truly a magnificent experience.

That child humbled me in a way I cannot explain. In that state, over the next few weeks, I witnessed one miracle after another. Those who couldn't see, saw. Those who couldn't walk, walked. I learned about the essence of healing: that if I didn't take credit and I didn't take blame, I could be in the zone that brought miracles to people.

When you're centered, you do not see yourself as separate from divinity *or* humanity, and you see human will and divine will as one.

That's when you have an inspired revelation that tells you what to do, and you act on it without reacting.

At the Institute of Heart Math in Boulder Creek, California, researchers have shown that when a person is in a state of love and appreciation, the power of their intent is maximized. The experimenters placed fragmented DNA in a beaker and had a person in that state concentrate on it from a distance. Microscopic examination showed that many of the DNA strands had been altered—just by *thinking.* They demonstrated that love and appreciation can affect matter from a distance, bringing order to our physiology and power to our intents.

Bi-aural Fusion

Because our physical senses are bipolar and dualistic, they need some sort of imbalance to function. Our senses are preprogrammed to perceive a world that is unbalanced and asymmetrical, and they can't detect anything else. Our fingers cannot feel without a contrast between texture or temperature, and we can't see in a pure white snowstorm or a pitch-black cave; there must be some differentiation.

But there's a phenomenon in physiology called bi-aural fusion that occurs in states of perfect balance. Say you hear a sound on your right side at a certain distance and location, and another sound on the left side in the exact yet opposite symmetrical position with the first sound. If they hit the same frequency, decibel level, distance, and angle, your brain cannot differentiate between the two. Your ears stop functioning and you experience bi-aural fusion, a core state like an inner voice. The same phenomenon can occur with any of your senses; resulting in bi-aural, bi-visual, or bi-kinesthetic fusion. In those states, the inner voice, the inner vision, and the inner feeling dominate the outer senses.

When we focus and bring our minds to perfect symmetry, the inner world is birthed—an inner attention, an inner presence. Magical things occur: Genius is awakened, art is created, and inspirational writing pours forth. That state is perfectly possible for all of us, but we don't have access to it as long as we take credit and blame and get elated and depressed—because of lopsided or asymmetrical perceptions—that's our mortal nature, and it covers up our immortal nature.

Our objective is to discover the underlying perfect symmetry, balanced proportion, and harmonious order, and allow the inner voice to become greater than the outer voices. That happens every time we merge our two sides into one, our emotional particles into light, and our personas into our true being—the soul.

The World Is a Mirror

An East Coast gentleman and his wife came to The Breakthrough Experience in Houston. The wife was a bit infatuated with me and my work, but the husband didn't want to be there—he resented me and thought the whole idea of the seminar was ridiculous. However, she had threatened to leave him if he didn't come. He spent the first few hours in the back of the room talking on his cell phone. At the end of the first night, she came up to me and said, "Dr. Demartini, I'm so sorry and *so* humiliated that my husband is so rude. I apologize for bringing this moron here."

He looked at her in absolute fury, then suddenly leapt up and came to the front of the room, his cell phone still in his hand, and barked at me, *"You stupid ass!* You have *no* idea who you are or what you're talking about; you have no background in what you're doing. You're not a psychologist, you're not a psychiatrist, you're not a scientist . . ." and for more than *30 minutes* he attacked me.

As fast as he screamed out his accusations, I did my best to own, equilibrate, and Collapse any charges. "You don't know what you're talking about. You're deceitful. You're scum. You're a thief. You're a liar." With every one of them, I was thinking, *Yes, that's true, in some way, at some time, in some manner, I display all those traits.* I had been and done them all in some form or fashion.

Finally, he calmed down and said, "That was my stuff, wasn't it?" And he said, "I think you're my father."

"I think so, too."

"That's the first time I've ever been able to get that out where he didn't beat me and chase me and threaten my life. Yeah, you were my father."

He did The Quantum Collapse Process on his father, and he opened his heart and just *bawled* for at least 25 minutes. Afterward, his wife stood up and put her arms around him, and they cried together.

As we finished the seminar, I asked if anyone had anything they'd like to say, and the wife said, "That's the first time I've ever seen my husband open up his heart." He nodded his head and said, "I think that's the first time in my entire *life* I've ever opened up like that. I don't even know how to explain what I've just been through."

She said, "You've helped me fulfill a dream. I didn't really want to leave my husband; that was a persona. I just wanted to know that he loved me, and right now I *know* he loves me."

Out of that entire class, the man who was *most* resentful became the most present. That angry man probably contributed more to me than anybody else there. He gave me the greatest gift—to know that no matter what he said about me, I could love myself. Is that a gift? To have people just attack the hell out of you, know that it's all true, in one form or another, and find out that you can still love yourself for it? Yes, that's the gift of The Quantum Collapse Process.

Everybody has two sides. If you're honest, you'll see that you are both saint and sinner, virtuous and vicious. So when someone accuses you of something, don't waste time defending yourself. Instead, admit that you are in fact possessor of whatever it is they're attacking you for. Not only are *you* possessor, but they are, too, and they're judging themselves; that's why they're accusing you. If it hurts to hear it, that means you haven't seen how that quality serves you or others and you're judging yourself. Their gift to you is to wake you up to another part of yourself that you haven't yet loved.

The Big Prison

I was teaching a class in Toronto to about 175 people, and there was a lady there who was very high up in the Canadian Justice Department. When I said that every human being has two sides, she stood up and said, "I disagree. I know people who are evil to the bone, and there is not one ounce of good in them."

I said, "Can you think of somebody you think is absolutely evil, a terrible person?"

"Yes."

"This is someone in your prison, right?"

"Yes, an evil, *evil* man."

I had her come up to the blackboard and list all the terrible things he'd done. She wrote down 27 evil things, and then I asked her to find out where she had done those same things in her life. The first thing she had written was that he'd murdered somebody, and when we dug down into her life, we found that she was once so angry with a prisoner that she told him, "As far as I'm concerned, you do not exist. You're the scum of the earth, and you are *never* getting out of here." He committed suicide that same night, and she felt responsible for his death. Then she thought back on all the men who had committed suicide in her penitentiary. Many prisoners thought she herself was a murderer and often called her one as she walked by.

I made her find out where she had done every single one of the

27 things she condemned that man for, to the same degree, and as she found them, she became more and more humbled. Then I asked her for his positive traits, and when we came up with 27 positives, she sat there with tears in her eyes.

I then asked her, "Who in this room reminds you of the man you once condemned?" Somebody in the room reminded her of her prisoner, and she embraced him and cried. She told him, "I never realized how much you contributed to my life, but today I finally understand. The most meaningful aspect of my life, what I give everything to, the thing I get up for every morning and am known around the country for, is not in *spite* of you, but *because* of you. I never saw it until this day."

She set herself free from her own prison. Instead of vendettas and revenge, she now wanted to make a shift in reform by bringing some of these ideas to the prison. She figured that if some people were going to spend their entire lives there, maybe she could help them learn to love themselves. She shifted her own perspective on how to deal with justice.

I said to her at the very end, "Do you realize that there is a divine justice going on, and no mortal can interfere with immortal justice? Just as this man took life, he has also given it to you. We're not here to judge another person; we're here to love."

> *"Whatever you do, you do to yourself.*
> *To judge others only compounds your own faults."*
> — The Buddha

I'm not saying that there aren't times when people definitely need to go to prison, I'm just saying that if we put them in prison and don't teach them how to love—and if we don't learn how to love *them*—they'll be back. But if you teach them how to love, they can transform their lives and make a difference.

We've all been in prison in some form: imprisoned by fear, guilt, doubt, uncertainty, and lack of clarity. Everybody deserves to be liberated, but we cannot have free will and freedom until we get beyond our illusions of infatuation and resentment. Just as we can be infatuated with somebody else for some quality or trait, we can also be infatuated with ourselves. If we let ourselves take credit, we will attract somebody to initiate us into taking blame.

Are You Absolutely Positive?

Society, religion, and some philosophies share a huge collective myth that one day we'll reach a point where our negative or dark side will disappear and we'll all be perfect, peaceful, and happy. This is not going to happen.

I went through a phase in my life when I was really into positive thinking. I read every book I could find. I was caught for years in the illusion of the one-sided, positive-thinking world. I would set out in the morning determined to be positive, but somewhere during the day, something would happen. The longer I stayed positive, the more something would blow, and I'd get really negative, either to myself or someone else. I noticed that the more I tried to put on the facade of being positive, the more I'd beat myself up inside. No matter what I did, I couldn't get rid of my negative side.

So I went to seminars.

One of the great proponents of the positive-thinking movement stood up one night in front of more than 1,000 people and said, "I'm probably one of the most negative-thinking people you've ever met." The whole room went *dead* silent, and his wife just nodded her head. "The reason I wrote the books on positive thinking was to balance out my negativity. I couldn't seem to function when I was so negative, so I needed to do something." He had helped to create an entire movement dedicated to being positive when he knew *he* certainly wasn't.

There is elated positive thinking and depressed negative thinking, and right between the two is *present* and loving thinking. The two extremes cancel each other out, and one is the antidote for the other. So does positive thinking have a place? Yes! From depression up to the center, it is wise to think positively. Does negative thinking or healthy skepticism have a place? Yes, from manic elation down to the center, you have to be a negating skeptic. Is anybody a skeptic? No. Is anybody a positive thinker? No. Is everybody *both*? Yes.

People who try to be positive to *everybody*, at home and in the world, end up negating themselves. You cannot get rid of the positive and negative balance. If you try to put on a facade for the world about how positive and upbeat you are, there will be chaos in your private life or your personal health.

The ancient Greeks knew that they had the power to heal and would bring the sick on stretchers to see plays for that very reason. Tragedy heals self-righteous people; it humbles them back down into their hearts. Comedy heals self-wrongeous people by lifting them back up into their heart. Nature knows this; the divine order uses both humiliating and pride-building circumstances to make sure you don't stray too far from your heart. You're not the victim, you're the creator of your own healing process, and you determine how long it takes by how quickly you get the lesson.

I once saw one of my positive-thinking heroes in Atlanta, Georgia. As he was about to speak in front of a packed room, his microphone failed, and he got *pissed*. The room was crowded, somebody was *sitting* on his notes, he had no microphone, and finally he just blew up!

He said, "What kind of *f——g* place is this? This is ridiculous!" and he stormed out of the place, screaming, leaving everyone in shock.

My hero!

When he did that, I thought, *Oh! Maybe when I'm negative . . . I'm not . . . without company.*

We're all negative at times, we're all both kind and unkind, with both a pleasant and an unpleasant side. I used to try to avoid half of it, but now I realize I don't need to do that. I want to love it so I know when to *use* it. You're given all your balanced qualities for a reason—to help you manifest your destiny—but anything you have a negative charge on you'll repress, and anything you embrace you can use to your advantage as a master.

I know this will challenge some belief systems, because the paradigm today says we're "supposed to be" upbeat and positive, but there's something out there that's much greater than that. Another major guru of the positive-thinking movement later said publicly that one of the most devastating things he ever did in his life was to get into the positive-thinking business. It just about shattered his relationships and caused all kinds of health issues and challenges in his family dynamic, because it put false expectations on a reality that demands two sides.

You're not here to be a one-sided being; you're here to embrace both sides of yourself. When you try to be one-sided, you expect other people to be the same, and when they aren't, you get angry with yourself, them, or the world. We're here to be whole beings, and positive and negative are the two sides to teach us that.

Never Say Never

About six years ago, at The Breakthrough Experience in the Midwest, a lady in the group swore self-righteously, "I would *never* get a divorce, *never* have an abortion, and *never* have an affair."

When I hear people say, "I would never do that," I write it down and put it in a sealed envelope and say, "Don't open this for six months."

Five months later, she came to another seminar and described her situation. "The last time I saw you, I swore I would never do some things, but a few months later, my husband had an affair that hurt me and made me so *angry*. I felt betrayed and trapped." She didn't want a divorce, but she couldn't stand to stay with him if he was going to continue his affair. She ended up having a little fling herself, got pregnant, and was considering having an abortion. That lady had been judging all the women in the world who got divorced and had affairs or abortions—she had closed her heart to all of them and thought she was superior—until it happened to her. Now she understood.

> *"Our deepest fears are like dragons,*
> *guarding our deepest treasure."*
> — Rainer Maria Rilke

Life is like a big play, and whatever role we most resist is the one we get to act in next. We draw in those things to teach us to love ourselves and the world. We're not here to judge, or be positive or negative thinkers; we're here to be *love* that embraces both sides.

The putting down and the lifting up are both love, and we're constantly getting both simultaneously, but we'll quickly become aware of whichever one we most need to bring us back to our center. Our self-righteousness resists and resents these events, but they *are* love, and they're here to bring us back to our true self-worth and heart; and when we get the lesson, they momentarily disappear.

We usually show strangers only one side of our nature at a time, and they either like or dislike us depending on which half-truth we reveal. We show friends more of both sides, and they have a deeper relationship with us—more understanding, patience, and appreciation. We show our spouses or partners almost *everything*, and what is the result? They love us most of all! The more we edit ourselves, the more like and dislike we receive from others; and the more we reveal our whole true self, the more we are loved.

Ultimately, life is not meant to be only positive or negative, happy or sad, but to be expressed with a balanced expression of love and wisdom. Wisdom is the instantaneous recognition that crisis is blessing, and love is the automatic, instantaneous expression of the two sides of life. You express either pure unconditional love when you acknowledge the balance, or conditional and emotional love when you acknowledge the imbalance. Either you're centered in a state of love, which feels most purposeful here on Earth, or you go off on emotional "tangents" to gain wisdom about what you haven't yet loved. You can't blow it. There are no mistakes. Tangents aren't detours, only reminders of how to grow in love.

If everything you did, said, and thought was broadcast 24 hours a day on eternity television, and everyone knew everything about you, could you love yourself? That's what this book is about—reaching such understanding and wisdom that even when you put yourself up or put yourself down, you just return to the truth of love. Every single person has *stuff*, things they're ashamed of and don't want to lay out on the table; that's called your private life. Mastery is the ability to take your privates public. By that, I mean that if you can take the private things you don't like about yourself and embrace them to the point where it doesn't matter if people find out about them or not, then you love yourself. When you love yourself, people can't push your buttons, but they will automatically attack you in whatever areas you attack yourself.

Everything you do, good or bad, positive or negative, serves to teach you about love. When you give yourself permission to be fully human, you approach the divine. But there are beliefs and misunderstandings that keep you from appreciating divinity in every aspect of yourself and the world. We'll deal with those in the next chapter.

Exercise 1

This simple exercise will reveal your self-righteous side. Collect a little saliva in your mouth, then put it in your hand and hold it away from yourself. Wave it around a little until it cools, and then put it back in your mouth. How does it feel? Pretty revolting?

I call this the Law of the Spit: The farther away in space and time the spit goes from your body, the less you're attracted to it. In fact, it almost approximates somebody else's spit. Why? Because you have a psychological boundary that thinks anything *out*side you is not as good as anything *in*side you. Your illusion that you are separate from the world is the basis of the myth of separateness: self versus other, good versus evil. Interesting?

Exercise 2

We normally look for differences between ourselves and others. This exercise is designed to reverse that. Sit in a public place where you have a great view of passersby, and start identifying yourself in them. Look quickly from person to person, and whatever trait stands out, ask yourself where and when you have the same quality. Find out where and when you're exactly like them.

Some traits are difficult to identify, particularly the ones you're charged about, but with practice, they become easier to see. As you improve, you'll be able to find yourself in anyone and anything. For example, a tree: "We are both made out of the substance of the earth; we are both life-forms that exist in time and space; we need light to live; we have seasons of growth and retreat; we carry microorganisms and couldn't live without them."

Eventually, your perceptions of good and bad or right and wrong will begin to fade, and you'll see just living beings. The longer you practice, the more the invisible walls come down, and you won't see the distance but the oneness between yourself and the world.

Words of Wisdom and Power

- *I am a human being. I have every trait in perfect balance, and they all serve.*
- *Whatever I see is me.*
- *Whatever appears, I look for the other side and am free.*
- *I take no credit and take no blame.*
- *This, too, is a lesson in love.*
- *Thank you for my skills and opportunities to participate in this world.*

Chapter Five

Who's Minding the Store?

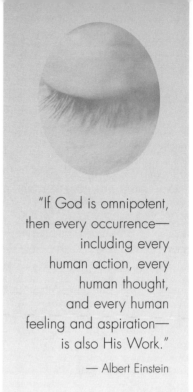

"If God is omnipotent, then every occurrence— including every human action, every human thought, and every human feeling and aspiration— is also His Work."

— Albert Einstein

O ur myths of one-sided triumphs and disasters keep us from recognizing divine order, and one of the biggest myths of humankind is the subject of death. It provokes perceptions of fear, pain, and suffering on Earth, yet it is simply another *illusion*.

From the fossil record, we know of at least five major extinctions on this planet, cataclysmic events that wiped out tremendous amounts of life. Nearly 90 percent of all species on Earth were eliminated 560 million years ago. Again, about 90 percent of all species on Earth were gone 250 million years ago. It is believed that a comet the size of a small city struck the earth at a speed of 25,000 miles per hour 60 million years ago; it hit the Gulf of Mexico with such force that great chunks of Mexican crust have been found as far away as France, and it wiped out approximately 60 to 70 percent of all species on Earth at that time.

One of the greatest paleontologists of our time, Professor Stephen Jay Gould, was looking at a graph of these periodic extinctions when something occurred to him. He superimposed a graph of evolution over the extinction graph and was astonished to find that they matched perfectly. Every time there was a major extinction, the next level of life appeared; for example, the Mexico comet helped bring extinction to the dinosaur but spurred the existence of mammals.

Gould looked at his charts and said something to the effect of, "You'd have to be an *idiot* not to see this connection!" Nature has never extinguished a species, or a group of species, without birthing a new species that was fewer in number but greater in organization and/or consciousness. Without the death of the old, the new cannot appear.

Human social consciousness is split into two factions: technologists who want to go boldly into the future and are often blinded to the past, and ecologists who want to hold things back and keep to the old ways. The two equilibrate each other and are vital regulators on the speed of evolution; they're like the gas pedal and the brake on our evolutionary vehicle.

Ecologists say it's our moral duty to save plant and animal species from extinction, but rescuing other life-forms may keep humans from being born. There is a synchronicity in timing. When we're booming, we knock out species; and when we slow down, we save them. The conservation of life on this planet is equilibrated—it's a law of both paleontology and nature, and we can't break it. If we try to slow down technology and go back to nature, we stagnate and the plants and animals increase. If we speed technology up too much, then the lower life-forms die and upset the carbon dioxide-oxygen cycle, which wipes us out as well. That's divine order again. Technology and ecology are just the two equilibrated sides of consciousness, and they regulate the speed at which we evolve. They're both right, and they're both necessary.

Natural Order

The cycles of evolution and extinction show us that we don't need to worry about a few degrees of warming or melting ice caps and rising sea levels, because they've already happened hundreds of times over the life of the earth. The South American rain forests disappear every 12,000 years as part of a natural glaciation cycle; the whole region goes from rain forest to savanna to brushland to grassland to desert and back again. After every major war, there is a baby boom. For every loss of species, there is the birth of a greater species, and it's all part of the natural order.

The world is bigger than us and oscillates on a grand scale, but most people don't look at lengthy enough time frames to become aware of it. They misinterpret the oscillations as impending doom and try to fix what isn't broken; they try to balance what is already perfect. It's all perfectly *natural*, but we somehow think it's a mistake—and our fault.

We live in tremendous fear and guilt about our potential to destroy the planet, yet human beings have done absolutely nothing in comparison to what nature regularly does. The extinction events were catastrophes on an unbelievable scale. The comet that struck Mexico did so with a force equal to 10,000 times the power of the entire world's nuclear arsenal. With our short time frames and lack of understanding, we get frightened and try to fix things, but our very attempts to fix them are part of the order, and we don't even realize it. In our ignorance, we think that the world is out of balance, and we try to fix anything we're ignorant about, including ourselves.

When I fly over many of the western regions of the United States, I sometimes wonder why there are no movements to "save the deserts." Many of these once-barren regions are now covered with enough vegetation to change the earth's humidity and pollen levels, yet no one seems to see the global equilibrations. The growing desire to plant trees, plants, and flowers in some parts of the world are natural expressions compensating for or equilibrating the capitalistic desire to eliminate the rain forests.

Mother Nature already has the world in perfect equilibrium, and we cannot disrupt it. If we start to destroy things, we'll automatically reduce ourselves in the process and restore the equilibrium. We simply can't screw it up.

Nothing but Light

Once again, fear splits us into two complementary particles. The optimistic New Age people say, "The world is about to enter into the golden age of enlightenment. Christ is returning, and we'll all live happily ever after in bliss," while the pessimistic doomsday prophets say, "The end of time is upon us. The Antichrist has arisen and the world is about to end." These illusions have been around for at least 2,000 years, yet the deadlines just keep going by, don't they?

Eventually we're going to realize that everything is ordered by an Intelligence wiser and greater than we can imagine. Death is a naturally recurring part of the cycle of life; there is no life without death, and the greater the death, the greater the life. The first law of thermodynamics states that energy and matter are neither created nor destroyed; they are only changed in form. It's also called the Law of Conservation, and it means that nothing in life is ever lost or gained.

"The things we think are destroyed are now in a frequency that we've tuned out of; the things we think are created have come into a frequency that we're tuned in to, but there is actually no creation or destruction, just change in form."
— Buckminster Fuller

So nothing is created, and nothing is destroyed. You aren't born, you don't die—you *are*. You will manifest in many forms throughout your existence. Nothing is gained or lost. This is a completely new paradigm in psychology that's starting to shake the world and shift our thinking. Most people think they can have sorrow without joy, or joy without sorrow—they think they can gain or lose things. But the same principles of catastrophe leading to new life apply on a personal as well as a global level: We live in a full-quantum state.

There Is No Loss

I was giving a talk once when the subject of death came up, so I asked the man whose question it was if he would mind helping the group understand something profound, and he agreed. His brother had recently died, and he was in sorrow and grief about it, so I had him write down all the perceptions of loss he had around his brother. He'd lost the friendship, the nurturing, his hazel eyes, his smile, his brown hair, his jokes, his challenging style, playing ball with him . . . the man listed 25 traits until he couldn't think of any more.

I said, "All right, that's the loss. Now what are the gains since he died?" At first, he found that hard to see or admit, but he finally allowed himself to acknowledge one area where his life was actually better without his brother. He said, "Well, he was very self-destructive, and I was always having to take care of him and rescue him. I got the blame from the family when something went wrong," and that's when he opened up the gates and the hidden truths appeared. We found benefit after benefit until they balanced his negatives. He already felt less of a sense of loss, but the process was still incomplete. The next step was to find the transformation.

I asked him, "Where are the new forms of the things you miss? Who took on the joking?" He thought a bit and then said, "Well, my father took on some of it; a best friend showed up from nowhere; and TJ, my fiancée."

I went right down the list and asked him, "Where are these things in your life now? Who has hazel eyes? Who has brown hair? Who likes to challenge you now?"

"My God, it's TJ."

All of a sudden, he hit a point where he realized that every one of those traits was manifested in a new form; the *moment* his brother died, they showed up. When he realized that so many of them were in the woman he loved, he began to cry. He felt his brother's presence in the room.

I asked him to close his eyes and imagine speaking to his brother. He began to tell his brother all the things he hadn't said before he died. As he spoke, he came to one previous action that he felt some guilt over, so I asked him, "How did this action benefit your brother?" I explained to him that everything ultimately serves, so how was his action a service to his brother? After staring into space for a moment, he began to see some benefits and no longer felt as if he had to apologize for his actions. He completely opened his heart with love; his grief was over.

Bereavement, grief, and remorse are simply forms of uncommunicated love and gratitude. People feel sorrow not because someone has died, but because they didn't express their love when they had the chance. This man had cried and cried—not from sorrow, but from love—and told his imagined brother how much he loved and appreciated him.

I then asked him, "When you think about your brother's death, do you have any sense of loss whatsoever?" and he just shook his head.

"Where do you feel your brother now?"

"I feel him right here, in my heart."

When he left that night, he came up and gave me a big hug and said, in a kind of dazed but very moved state, "That was the strangest thing . . . my whole perception of my brother . . . now my appreciation for TJ . . . I realize why she's in my life now, because there is no loss."

I have taken *hundreds* of people through The Quantum Collapse Process to dissolve their grief. Not only have we consistently found what they thought they had lost, but they realized that they preferred the new form to the old one and wouldn't want to go back. The existing paradigm in psychology says that two to five years is the normal duration of the grieving process, and I certainly disagree with that belief system. It's possible to completely dissolve grief in *two to five hours* . . . through the power of love.

Life is too precious to spend on illusions of loss and death. Do not fall into the illusion of what some people call *compassion* by supporting the myth of loss. Care enough about them to find the equilibrium, and help them have communion of spirit with their loved one; in so doing, you will illuminate them.

You Want It? You've Got It!

If you were to write down everything you want in a partner, you might be surprised to find that it's already in your life right now; it's just not in a form that you've recognized. It may be split among several of your friends, relatives, and colleagues, but as long as you're ungrateful for the form it's in, you'll block it from manifesting into the form you think you want. Love it the way it is, and it will transform into the way you love. This is very powerful to understand. Nothing is missing.

I worked with a woman in Hollywood, California, who told me, "I haven't had sex in *six years*."

I said, "Are you sure that's true?"

"What do you mean am I sure it's true? I haven't had sex in six years. *I* ought to know."

"Let us look and see what form sex is in. What specifically do you think you have missed in relationship to sex? How do you define sex?"

"Well, it's somebody who's intimate with me and touches me, a look in the eye, a feeling . . . " We broke it down, and I asked where she was already getting each component.

"Where are you getting that intimate eye contact?"

"With one of my clients. We look at each other, and there's a kind of sexual innuendo or energy. It's not physical sex, but I can see that part is there. And there's something there with my business partner that we have to be a little careful about."

"And who is giving you the touch?"

She was an interior decorator specializing in bathrooms, kitchens, and vases, and we found out it was the sexual vases. She had male sexual objects all *over* the place! She'd put them somewhere and stroke them and turn them from side to side and look down the openings and then pick them up and rub them and put them somewhere else. Partly because she wasn't having physical sex, her whole successful career became a sublimated form of sexuality; all of her more successful designs, those that clients were most drawn to, were her sexually oriented pieces. Upon this realization, she became very grateful. She also realized that the last time she did have a physical sexual partner, her business significantly declined, interfering with her highest values of being independent and owning a successful company.

The instant people realize that they already have what they thought was missing, they're free, and they understand that they have the power to get it in whatever form they want. The person who feels desperate is the one who pushes away the new manifestation of the form they think they're missing. This woman realized that she didn't even want that form of sex; she just *thought* she did. If someone is having their sex in the virtual rather than the physical world, it's because they have a whole bunch of negatives attached to the physical form.

"It means I have to make a commitment, it takes me away from my business, I have to make decisions with somebody else, I have to spend my money, it can be messy and disruptive and emotionally painful, and . . ." Those underlying concerns were all wrapped up in her present reality, so she made sure it *didn't* show up in that form and *did* show up in the new form, because that was the one she really preferred. When she realized she had the power to manifest sex in any way, she had the option and could attract somebody if she wanted to.

One of the greatest discoveries I've made is that nothing is missing; it's always equilibrated, and we're always surrounded by whatever we love. Just as in a relationship, where the more you try to change your partner the more they resist you, the more you try to change the world into your fantasy of how it should be, the more it bites you. Love it for what it is, and you have the power to transform it—not because you *need* to change it any longer, but because love gives you the power to do so. Love is magic.

Four Great Questions

When we begin to experience illusions during our Earthly existence as the result of the dualistic senses of our bodies, we automatically separate these experiences into future and past states. Because we live in the future and the past rather than the present, we continually raise the four great questions of life, those that philosophy has attempted to answer throughout history: *Where have we come from? Where are we going? Why are we here? Who are we?*

Astronomy tells us that we come from stars and return to stars. When this local galaxy of stars came into being, it contained light, subatomic particles, hydrogen, and helium. Grains of cosmic dust and the gravitational and nuclear power of recycling stars created all the other heavier elements. We are made of star stuff, and in five billion years, when the sun enters its red giant phase, it will expand out beyond Mars, and anybody still here will be absorbed back into it. As we grow and develop our consciousness, we'll shine like stars in the darkness of ignorance, and eventually we'll come to realize that we never were anything else.

But most of us think very terrestrially, don't we? We live on this little planet and look out at the horizon. We stop at the earth. If we go out into space, we see the earth as a celestial body, and we look at humans from a different perspective. If we go to the edge of our solar system, we can't even *see* the earth anymore; we see the *sun*. What are we, then? We are astronomical, stellar people.

Some people say, "You know, I just want to take care of my *family* tonight. I'm not really concerned about where we're going to be in the next million years," but this is an important principle; the magnitude of space and time within your innermost dominant thought determines the level of conscious evolution you've obtained. The breadth of your vision determines the quality of your life, and the effect you have on the world.

There's a similar relationship between consciousness and time. The bum on the corner lives from hand to mouth, hour to hour, and day to day. The man selling pretzels on the same corner lives day to day and week to week. If you ask the beggar how it's going, he'll say, "It's been a bad day," or "It's been a good day," while the pretzel man says, "Ah, it's been a good week," or "It's been a bad week." The people who work in the corner shoe shop say, "It's been a great month," while the shop owner says, "It's been a fair year." The manager of a large department store will say, "We've had a couple of good years," but the store owner says, "We're going to be setting a trend over the next 25 years." The CEO has a bigger vision: "This is where we're headed in the next century."

And then you meet a sage, a wise being with a universal perspective, and what does he talk about? *Eternity*. He doesn't think in terms of mortal time and space; he thinks about forever.

I've been giving a program for five years on economics and finance that teaches people how to unfold their wealth. Your worth in life is directly proportionate to how much love and gratitude you have, and the hierarchy of your values and magnitude of your cause determines much of your wealth. A lot of people unconsciously sabotage their wealth-building because their values and beliefs make them feel unworthy, while those who have great causes and value wealth receive great prosperity.

You can't get beyond yourself without a cause greater than you. Every time you get clear about your mission and reduce your emotional static, your vision becomes clearer, your cause expands, and the magnitude of space and time within your innermost dominant thought grows and expands. As you expand yourself and your vision grows, your resources increase, and broader domains of space and time are yours to play in. You have a sphere of influence, and you also have a realm of resource; and as your influence increases, so does your resource. *Re-source* means to get back to the source. Stay with the inner heartfelt source and the resource is yours. Love and appreciation connect you to this true source of wealth.

The magnitude of space (how big your vision is) and time (how far you can see in the future and how much patience you have) determines the level of conscious evolution you obtain. Short-term pleasure leads to long-term pain, like overeating and getting fat, or watching TV every night and ending up with a life that doesn't fulfill your dreams. But the greater your vision and patience, the greater your power and scale of creation. A child wants immediate gratification, while an adult has hopefully learned some patience. When you're 70 years old, a year is no big deal, is it? It's like a day, but to a child, one day seems like a year.

> *"The stock market is a financial redistribution system.*
> *It takes money away from those who have no patience*
> *and gives it to those who have."*
> — Warren Buffet

And what opens up consciousness? You see, your immortal soul is vast; it doesn't have a limited consciousness. But the mortal part of you is based on a limited time-event horizon, and this horizon is in the future or the past depending on your perception. If your perceptions are finite, you see things locally; but if you're more patient and your vision approaches the infinite, you see things nonlocally. In other words, you could be standing on the earth saying, "This is terrible! Look at that awful devastation," while on the opposite side of the planet is some magnificent, terrific experience. No wonderful event happens anywhere in the world without a terrible anti-event that exactly balances it in magnitude. The sage sees the whole earth simultaneously and says, "Thank you."

What I'm offering is the awareness that in all events of life, there is this nonlocal, equilibrating anti-event. That's where the mystery is; that's where the magic is; and that's where your mission, love, and heart are. Your spirit is trying to tell you that everything is balanced, but your senses give you lopsided perceptions. You evolve by finding the balance in all things and acknowledging the Intelligence greater than yourself that governs it.

It's All about Perspective

About 20 years ago, I was going through what I believed to be a tough time. I had been in practice for about a year and had just spent a lot of money to expand my office space and buy new equipment. I'd bought a new home and car and was being audited by the IRS. I was about to get married, so I had a honeymoon to Hawaii and two diamond rings to pay for. In addition, my soon-to-be wife had a son from a previous marriage, so I was also taking on that responsibility. I'd hired two new staff members and a new doctor, but my practice suddenly dropped to 20 percent of what it had been. I felt really stressed, and went out to see my father. We were sitting in the front yard, and he asked me, "How's it going, son? You look a little tense."

"I'm stressed as hell, Dad."

"What's going on?"

So I went through the whole list and said, "I'm totally overwhelmed. It's like it all hit me at once."

I wanted him to say, "Gee, son, you poor thing. Boy, you're strong! I couldn't handle all that," but he didn't. Instead, he said, "Son, don't you realize what you have? Your mother and I have been married for 32 years and we never got to go on a honeymoon, and you're going to Hawaii, the dream place we always wanted to see. You have a bigger home and more cars right now than we have after all that time. We only had gold bands; I never got to give your mom a diamond until I was in business for 25 years. You already have a beautiful son who's healthy. You have a great office that you're expanding—at least you've made money to pay taxes on—you're hiring and employing people, and you have one of the fastest-growing practices in Texas. You're marrying someone you love and going on a dream trip and growing your business—you're doing more in your first year than I did in 32 years. That doesn't sound like stressings to me, son; it sounds like *blessings*. I wish I was in that boat."

When he said that, I thought to myself, *Hmm! Maybe it's just a perspective game.* There *is* a balance, and sometimes we stress because we deny the other side. Everything that happens is just an event that, if taken out of context, could be seen as terrible or terrific. There is pleasure with every pain, and they're exactly equal. The bigger the pain, the bigger the pleasure that comes with it. We're going to get both no matter what we do, so it might as well be in the pursuit of our dreams.

The Aging Process

I wrote a book 23 years ago on the perceptions and illusions of the mind and how they affect the aging process and disease in the body, and I'm convinced that every time we fail to see the divine order, we age. I'm also convinced that every time we see the divine order, we become present, and space and time dissolve. Now, we don't stay there; we go from one experience to the next and have our illusions about life, and therefore we age. We're not going to stop the aging process except for moments, but those moments of presence are ageless. That's when we acknowledge the infinite and eternal present. We're infinitely attuned; and we inwardly see, hear, and feel holistically.

We grow through ever-greater spheres of influence and outreach, and we cannot rule or govern that which we haven't transcended. To transcend is to master, and mastery is based upon loving and understanding the duality within any concentric sphere. I believe that if we want to make a difference in ourselves, we must have a vision at least as big as our family. To make a difference in our family, we must have a vision as big as our city. We must have a vision as big as the state to make a difference in our city, and a vision as big as the nation to make a difference in our state. We must have a vision as big as the globe to make a difference in our nation, and it takes an astronomical vision to make a global difference.

Those who don't have astronomical visions are unlikely to make global impacts. The benefit of investigating the astronomical domains is to expand our human consciousness, to see ourselves outside the terrestrial sphere, to realize that we're celestial beings having temporary Earthly experiences instead of thinking that we're terrestrial beings having occasional spiritual visions. We are vastly *bigger* than that. To have a global impact, we must look out at the world and see the whole picture in terms of astronomy, geology, and evolution, not stand here looking at ourselves and feeling small.

One answer to the four great questions is that we are stars, but love and light are equally true answers. The universe is an infinite school of unending spiritual light. We're here to learn, teach, and become our true nature, love and light, and those closest to us are our greatest teachers *and* students in this school of life.

Exercise

This is an extremely powerful exercise to help you transcend the myth of loss or death:

1. Think of someone you believe you "lost" at some time in your life, through change, divorce, or death. Write down the specific traits or aspects you think you lost.

2. Go back to that exact time and place, and ask yourself, "What were the new forms of these specific traits or aspects? How did those qualities immediately show up in my life in some other form?" As you discover them, write down the new form that each quality appeared in.

You may have to be creative and insightful to recognize the new form. The qualities you miss in someone may appear in other people, yourself, a beloved animal, or new relationships and opportunities. They can also manifest in the virtual reality of your memory, imagination, and dreams.

3. It's not a matter of *if* the new forms exist; it's simply a matter of *where* they exist, so don't stop looking until you find them. You'll know you're done when you realize that you wouldn't exchange the new form for what seemed lost. When you see the blessings, you'll experience a moment of silence and stillness, and a tear of inspiration.

Words of Wisdom and Power

- *I look at great spans of time, and see great order.*
- *In love, there is no loss.*
- *There is a vast intelligence running the world, and it is in order.*
- *Death is an illusion; life just changes form.*
- *I have a great vision, and money flows in to help me fulfill it.*
- *There is nothing to fix, but much to love.*

Chapter Six

Relationship

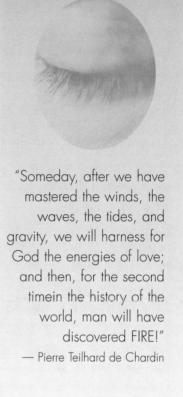

"Someday, after we have mastered the winds, the waves, the tides, and gravity, we will harness for God the energies of love; and then, for the second timein the history of the world, man will have discovered FIRE!"
— Pierre Teilhard de Chardin

Between extreme particles is a center point of light. Between extreme emotions is the center point of love. The center point is what every human being already is, yet elusively still seeks. True love is our ultimate objective, whether we're aware of it or not. We may think we're looking for something else, something material and fleeting, but even the pursuit of transient goals just leads us back to the truth of love. The purpose of all relationships is to dissolve the barriers that keep us from recognizing the love that already is, and expressing the love we ultimately are.

Every human being you'll ever have a relationship with will at times be nice and mean, supportive and challenging, pleasureful and painful, attractive and repulsive. The purpose of relationship isn't happiness; it's a combination of happiness and sadness, which makes up fulfillment. If we seek happiness, we're only looking for half-fillment; and if we seek sadness, we're looking for the other half-fillment. When we look for fulfillment, we appreciate both sides.

Don't you have times in your relationship when you're happy and times when you're sad? If you think something's wrong with your relationship because you have sadness half the time, you're missing out on the big picture, because that's the way it's designed. The sadness just means your buttons are being pushed and you're seeing the parts of yourself that you haven't loved yet.

Buttons are nothing but lopsided perceptions, and people come into your life as teachers to point them out to you. The ones who push your buttons the most are your greatest teachers. If you can bring your lopsided perceptions back into balance, you'll appreciate them as your teacher; if you can't, you'll blame them for being a button-pusher. As you grow in wisdom, you'll learn to embrace and love others for who they are, looking for the benefits they offer you and knowing that they represent parts of you that you've buried or disowned. Wisdom means thanking others for bringing to your awareness those areas where you've lied and not loved, and for being grateful that they've given you this opportunity to love.

700 Hearts

Your relationships with others are simply mirrors of your relationship with yourself. Anything you have loved in yourself you can embrace in the world.

I once had the opportunity to speak to 700 high school students, and I shared with them stories of my own teenage years on the streets, hitchhiking and living in bowling alleys, communes, and tents. Many speakers who came to this school didn't really relate to the students, but I told them my life story, and they related to it. I talked about not fitting in and experimenting with all the things teenagers do. I shared that I'd been interested in sex and all those daring activities just like they were. I expressed how I came to love it all because it made me who I am today. I got right into their world and told them how normal, and yet at the same time, extraordinary, they were. I spoke about what was inside them. I had them all in tears, 700 teenagers sitting in a big hall crying. They wanted to find their mission and live their dreams.

Teachers came up to me after my speech and said, "I didn't even know my kids had such feelings. How did you get hundreds of kids to not say one word, or even move, for more than an hour?"

I said, "When you can't wait to share a message from your heart, your students can't wait to hear it."

Paul Bragg helped me identify my mission when I was 17. I made a commitment to myself then that I would do the same thing when I'm 93 for some 17-year-old. In the meantime, I'd practice on all the people I could. After talking to those teenagers, I received dozens of profound and touching thank-you letters. I tried to read some of them at a seminar weeks later, but I got so choked up that someone else had to do it for me, because my dream was coming true.

Inside every single person is an overwhelming desire to fully express their divinity, the absolute spirit of love that they have and are. Sometimes we go through life and bang our heads against the wall because we can't figure out how to express our divinity. We rationalize and lie to ourselves that it's not meant to be, that we don't know what it is, that we don't really want it or we're satisfied the way we are. The only thing that truly satisfies the soul is love and appreciation, and when we feel and express these feelings, we feel fulfilled.

The Purpose of Marriage

Many people still live with the illusion that the purpose of marriage is happiness. This fantasy apparently began in the 12th century when the troubadours created romantic love. Marriage is not about happiness, unless you redefine the term *happiness* as fulfillment, which is the synthesis of both positive and negative emotions. Marriage was never intended to be one-sided. In the marriage vows, we pledge to love for richer and poorer, in sickness and in health, for better and for worse.

Understanding the purpose of marriage can free you from an extremely pervasive myth that is the source of many marriage breakups. The purpose of marriage is to teach people how to fully love themselves, their owned and disowned parts. Love is the perfect equilibrium of pain and pleasure, support and challenge, nice and mean, pleasant and unpleasant, like and dislike. In any relationship, except during moments of presence and unconditional love, you'll oscillate between liking and disliking the person as you fluctuate around the center point of love. Love is not a static state that we reach and then stop; it is a constantly growing and expanding force.

Both sides, pleasure and pain, make up the dynamic called *love*. If you have a fantasy that love is only supposed to be one-sided, you'll reject half of love and won't embrace the whole experience. In fact, physical lovemaking is actually pushing someone away half the time and wanting them to come close the other half. It involves a pendulous motion of away, close, away, close, away, close, gradually increasing in speed until you climax. Imagine if it only consisted of pushing or pulling away. Nothing would happen; you'd be stuck.

Imagine if you were dating someone or married to someone who always said, "I think you're wonderful. You're always right. You're unbeatable the way you are." If all they did was support, support, support you, you'd do whatever you could to confront and challenge them. In fact, Mr. or Ms. Nice automatically develops the doormat syndrome—people walk all over them until they say, "Hey, I'm worthwhile, too, and I'm not going to keep exaggerating *your* worth." Someone who receives only support will eventually say, "This isn't working. I need somebody who can stand up to me. I want some *challenge*."

There are times when it's important to be soft, and times when it's vital to be tough. If you don't understand that love has both sides, you'll feel loved only when your mate is nice, and unloved when your mate isn't. I'll play hardball with my wife sometimes for that reason, because I know that if I get too soft, she'll get too hard; and if I get too hard, she'll get too soft, and she's wise enough to do the same for me. If you just keep yelping, they'll come down on you; sometimes you have to roar back. That's the *game*. Master it.

People who say, "I don't want to play games in relationship," are constantly at the mercy of the game. When you play the game and master the rules, embracing the challenges of life, you'll get more mastery over your life.

The 12-Year Itch

A man once called me from Boston and said, "I'm having problems with my relationship." He was comparing his wife to another woman and to a moment of assumed pleasure he'd had 12 years ago. "This other woman and I were together for three days, and it was unbelievably passionate, but my present wife isn't quite as passionate, and I don't have the same feeling for her. We've been together now for eight years, and it's just not the same."

He couldn't appreciate what he presently had as long as he compared it to the fantasy. He wasn't present; he was living in the past, and that so-called past pleasure and his present pain were a team.

So I asked him, "What was the pain of that lady 12 years ago?" but he could only say, "Man, she was *beautiful*." He was totally infatuated with her body, but I kept asking him to find her negative traits until he finally got it. He saw the obsession; the pain of losing her; and her vanity, self-absorption, and promiscuity. He remembered the high maintenance and the lack of a deeper meeting of minds. He had compared her to every relationship he ever had and found fault with them all, leaving wonderful women over and over again because they didn't measure up to that one fantasy experience. He thought about her for years, which resulted in his not really being there for his wife. Finally, after working The Quantum Collapse Process with him, I helped him balance it all out and dissolve his illusion.

He then saw that the negatives and positives were equal, and at that *moment*, he started appreciating his wife. He realized that she gave him different forms of comforts and pleasures, and the negatives he felt about her were balanced by the positives, reawakening him to her beauty and love. Suddenly he was crying tears of appreciation for his wife, and he got *present* with her, freeing himself from a fantasy that had controlled his life and kept him from seeing the wonderful woman who loved him.

I told him that if you're not satisfied with your partner, it may be because you're comparing them to some fantasy. You've created a myth that they're supposed to live up to, a hidden agenda that you haven't even communicated, and when they fail to live up to it, you punish them. Your fantasy is all positives and no negatives, which doesn't exist, and you beat them up for their negative side, which is exactly what you need to grow. Your mate is magnificent, but as long as you have the myth, you won't have a present relationship. You must destroy the myth of relationships to experience the truth of love.

Ah, Passion!

The Law of Conservation states that nothing is built in the universe without something else being destroyed, and I haven't seen it violated yet. Have you ever gone walking with your loved one through a public park and seen a beautiful couple on a bench kissing with real passion and intimacy? You've been married for 20 years and you're not even holding hands, but you see them and think, *What happened to the passion we had? What happened to us?* When two people see passion, they often pull away from each other and wonder what's wrong with their relationship.

But if you see two people sitting on that bench fighting and screaming and really having it out, you draw together, hold hands, and exchange pitying looks about the poor devils who don't have the love you do.

I consult with a lot of people who say, "We don't have that kind of passionate relationship anymore, and we really want it," but they don't realize what happens when you get that passion back. If you walk past the bench again and see that same passionate couple two hours later, guess what they're doing? Fighting! *Screaming* at each other sometimes. Do you remember the passionate, immature phase of your relationship? The two sides of emotion come together as pairs, and resentment is the price of infatuation. For everything that comes together, something else goes apart. It's the law.

> *"Being deeply loved by someone gives you strength,*
> *while loving someone deeply gives you courage."*
> — Lao Tzu

You *can* have a realistic view of marriage and go into it with a balanced understanding. It's called the *true* marriage vows: for better and for worse, for richer and for poorer, in sickness and in health. The vows tell you in advance that love is not all pleasure, but most people don't understand until they've lived it. When you embrace both sides, you can truly embrace the whole person.

Your Value Systems

Did you know that you're run by your value systems? We all have a hierarchy of values, from the things we think are extremely important, all the way down to the things we think don't matter. Your values dictate your destiny. Anything that supports your highest values you call "good" and are attracted to; anything that challenges them you call "bad" and are repelled by.

Your values are based on the perception that something is missing, that a void exists. But the Law of Conservation says that nothing is missing, it's just in a form you haven't recognized. You think you're missing it; therefore, you seek it, and anything you think supports that search you call good and anything that challenges it you call "bad."

If, just before I leave for a month's tour of different European cities, I go up to my wife and say, "Honey, I'll be gone for a month. See you when I can, call you if I get a chance. Bye, babe," do you know what she'll say as I'm about to leave?

"I don't think this relationship's working. You don't love me. I may not be here when you get back." This response wouldn't be surprising, because I'm not talking in her values, am I?

But what will happen if I say, "Honey, I'm going on a world tour. I'll be securing our future by earning a substantial bit of money, and I wonder if you can meet me in Venice one month from today for the next full moon. I'd like to take a gondola down the Grand canal in the moonlight, listen to the violins, and then look at some beautiful jewelry and go clothes shopping. We can get massages every day, relax, enjoy the sun, have some great dinners, and make love for hours a day. Is there *any* way you can meet me in Venice?"

She's going to say, "I love you, honey. Thank you for working so hard. You're such a wonderful husband. I can't wait to see you there. I'll make all the arrangements, don't worry."

One scenario met her values; the other completely challenged them. If I don't honor my wife by knowing her values, and if I don't know *my* values and learn how to communicate them in terms of hers, then I don't know how to care about her.

My wife does the same thing with me. She'll say, "John, we're having dinner again tonight at the finest and most expensive restaurant in New York City." If she simply says we're going to dinner there, I see money disappearing; and another heavy, rich meal, but if she says, "We're going out to dinner with the head of a major corporation who's looking for a professional speaker to address his organization. I'm not sure, but I think it may be a new business opportunity for you," guess what I'll say?

"Absolutely. No problem. Let's go!"

She thinks and talks in terms of my values if she wants me to do something, and I'll talk in terms of her values if I want *her* to do something. The things we say are true, so are we lying to each other? No, we're *caring*. The opposite would be an uncaring relationship: trying to push your values onto someone else, trying to get them to do what you do and live your values.

There are three ways to conduct a relationship, and each one has an entirely different outcome. A careless relationship is one in which you project and focus on your own values without considering your partner's at all. A careful relationship is when you think in terms of their values without considering your own—this one is called "walking on eggshells." Both are one-sided approaches that ignore the other person and create tension in the relationship. But a caring relationship is one where you communicate your values in terms of theirs. You think of both sides simultaneously, expressing your love for yourself and each other. The definition of caring is knowing someone well enough to know their values, and caring enough to express your values in terms of theirs.

No matter how much I try to communicate in terms of my wife's values, there are going to be times when I'm more focused on my own. That means I'm going to betray and challenge her at times; she's not going to like or trust me at times, and she'll even resent me, and that's *normal*. I have my individuality, too, and I can't sacrifice my life totally for her. The more I sacrifice myself for her, the more she'll minimize me because I'm minimizing myself. She'll take me for granted and treat me accordingly. But if I can find a balance between support and challenge where she grows maximally, and she can find a balance of support and challenge where I grow maximally, we have a more fulfilling relationship. She stands up and goes against me at times, and she stands with and for me at times. That's a well-balanced relationship.

Home Rules

Whenever something supports your values; you take away the rules, and when something challenges your values, you set rules. Nations do it, companies do it, and you do it in relationships. You set up rules when your values feel threatened.

One time I was playing with my children, roughhousing, screaming, and having fun. Suddenly an important business call came in. One of my highest values? Succeed in business and make money. The children were still hollering when I grabbed the phone, and I couldn't hear the caller, so what did I say to the kids? "Stop that! I told you to quit roughhousing in here," even though I was just doing it with them two minutes before.

"Stop yelling and screaming in the house. Go to your room!" Who's yelling and screaming now? I am.

"Go to your room! That's the rule!" and then politely back to the phone. "Hello?"

Often when we're in a relationship, we unwisely think the other person is supposed to be like us, and we project our hierarchy of values onto them. When they support our values, we call them "good" and let them do almost anything they want. But when they challenge our values, we suddenly call them "bad" and clamp down with our laws, rules, and ultimatums.

We want them to be like *us*, but as I said earlier, if any two people are exactly the same, one of them is unnecessary. Two people in marriage typically try to project their values onto their mate, but if they ever succeeded, they would destroy the relationship. The purpose of marriage is to teach us to love the parts we've disowned, so 50 percent like them and 50 percent unlike them is the ideal reality.

Not too long ago, a lady said to me, "My husband treats me like *dirt*. He treats me terrible."

So I asked her, "Where does he treat you terrifically?"

"He doesn't, he treats me terrible."

"Yes, but listen carefully to what *I'm* saying. Where does he treat you terrifically?"

When she finally understood what I meant, I spent an hour drawing terrifics out of her. She finally got enough terrifics to balance out the terribles, and she sat there in loving tears.

She said, "I never saw it. I never saw that the way he showed me love was through *his* value system, not mine."

That's why there's *no such thing* as a trusting relationship 100 percent of the time. If a man has the values of money and business, when his finances or career are threatened, he'll spend time away from his family to take care of it. If the woman's highest values are family and children, she'll stay home from work when her kids are sick. I don't mean to stereotype. Of course there are couples whose roles are reversed, but this is a common pattern.

Each person has their own set of values, and no two people have the same set. They can live up to their values, but not to yours.

We impose our values on top of theirs 50 percent of the time and expect them to conform, and that's why we have conflict 50 percent of the time—to wake us up to what we're doing.

People show their love through their own value system and nobody else's—unless they're humble, wise, honorable, and caring enough to communicate in your values. But their natural inclination is to express love in terms of their own values. If a man's highest values are finance, intelligence, and career, he'll perceive that he's loving his family by making sure he supports them, succeeds in business, and is smart. In his mind, he'll be thinking, *I'm smart, and business is going well; I'm loving my family*, while his wife is thinking, *You don't love me because you're not taking care of the kids or making time for us to be alone together*. Those are *her* values. Meanwhile, he thinks she doesn't love him because she's not going out and getting a job to make money, or isn't interested in the same things he is.

Each person expresses love through their own values. When we honor their value systems, we realize that we're surrounded by love in forms we don't even recognize.

The Argument Field

Every human being has a domain, a territory that fluctuates according to their emotions. Arguments happen when two people in a relationship need to either add or subtract space, time, energy, or matter. Any perceptions of too much or too little of any of those elements will cause arguments to equalize them. Are arguments bad? No, they're telling you that somebody loves you and wants to regulate space, time, energy, and matter with you.

When you're in conflict, just ask yourself, *Am I giving too much or too little space, time, energy, or matter here?* When you find out which one it is and provide it, the argument will stop. It's surprisingly simple.

Did you know that everyone has a running checklist on their relationship with you? They have a complete log of every exchange from the time they met you until now, and you have the same with them. They know exactly where your exchange with them is, and when there's a conflict, out it comes. Remember that what they think is just what they think; it may or may not be accurate, and the argument is the process of sorting it out.

Sometimes they think they've given you a lot of attention (time) and want some back. Sometimes they feel they were there for you (space) and suddenly you're not available. Sometimes they bought or gave you something (matter) and expect you to reciprocate. Sometimes they've listened to you whine (energy), and now they want you to listen to *them* whine. These may seem like small things, but perceptions of imbalance have the power to close the heart.

Sometimes all somebody wants is to be left alone. If you leave them be, ten minutes later they can come in and hug you and want to be with you. Care enough to give them the space they need, and you'll get love in return. Sometimes they want you in their space, and when you're willing to just stop and be with them, the problem disappears. A moment of presence is more powerful than *hours* of impatient half-attention. Love is a chargeless field, unlimited or infinite. Give space and you get love; give love and you get space. Try it and see.

Most people live in the myth that to love someone is to never disappoint, upset, or hurt them. Do you know that the one you love is the one you initiate the feelings of hurt in half the time? I'm redefining "love." Most people think it's only the nice side and hate the mean side, but that's not true. When you love someone, you're the nicest *and* the meanest to them. You support and challenge, you're pleasant and unpleasant, you lift them up and put them down, you do things for them and ignore them. Those are the two sides of love.

The myth says that you're supposed to show only one side, but that creates tension in a relationship and in your life because it represses half of the truth. When I'm the toughest on my wife (and I am really tough on her sometimes), that's when she comes to me and thanks me the most. Sometimes I'll play the soft role, and she'll accumulate tension; and then when I play the hard role, she softens. She knows it, too, and she plays it back to me. We know the love game.

> *"Love does not consist in gazing at each other,*
> *but in looking together in the same direction."*
> — Antoine de Saint-Exupéry

Along with love, war is also an essential part of wholeness and well-being. Half the time you *need* a good war in your relationship. Conflict and competition are necessary for growth. We're not here to have only peace; we're here to have both sides of life's coin. So if you have a conflict in your relationship, don't think, *Uh-oh, my relationship is failing.* No, it's growing! It's challenging you, making you look at yourself. When you self-inspect, change your beliefs and the way you handle things, and learn how to master communicating in terms of the other person's values, you grow.

Have you ever tried to change somebody by taking a stance? What happens when you say, "Look, I'm right and you're wrong, and if you don't change, it's my way or the highway"? The more polarized and entrenched you become, the more they take the opposite stance and become polarized to you. When you both dig in, you end up with a stalemate. But what if you said instead, "What I see in you is a part of me. I have it inside myself, and by your pointing it out, I get an opportunity to appreciate a part of myself that has been unloved. It's serving me by bringing me humility because I was so cocky, and I appreciate you for being my teacher." Then you'd come to the center, and what would happen to the other person? They'd come to the center as well; if you're truly in your heart, they can't resist.

Love cannot be rejected, but expectation will certainly be. Most people confuse love with expectation. You can't avoid having expectations and opinions, but to get stuck in them is to stop your growth. The Breakthrough Experience was created to help you transcend your rigid opinions and birth love, and then dissolve your *next* opinions and birth love, and keep expanding as a human being.

Whatever you love turns into what you would most love it to be. If you try to fix or change somebody, they'll resist; but if you honor and thank them for who they are, *as* they are, and love them for who they are, they'll assist. When you love people for who they are, they turn into whom you love.

Crisis Is Blessing

A lady once came to The Breakthrough Experience because she was having problems in her marriage. She said, "I've been seeing another man for eight years. My husband doesn't know about it, but we've really had problems since we were married. I think even at the marriage ceremony I didn't really want to be with him, but I didn't have the courage to speak up because of the social pressures, and I didn't trust my intuition."

I asked her, "So what would you truly love to do? What's true for you?"

"I'm afraid of what people will think about me if I leave. I'm afraid of what will happen to my kids, I'm afraid about the finances . . ."

She had *30* fears wrapped around her relationship, and we Collapsed as many of them as we had time for. She Collapsed the fear of telling her husband about the affair, her infatuation with the boyfriend, the fear of what people would think or say, the money—as many fears as she could think of.

Then she went home and told her husband some of her previous actions and present feelings. She felt it was best to not reveal all the details immediately, but she said to him, "I'm going to be truthful to myself about our relationship and move on." He was shocked and became furious.

He said to her, "You go to this seminar, and you *leave* me," then he got on the phone and cussed me out, saying, "Well, Dr. Demartini, *thank you very much*. You just destroyed my relationship."

I asked him, "Can you help me understand what you mean by that?"

"My wife just told me that she's leaving me because she went to your seminar."

"Do you know what actually happened there?"

"No, but whatever it was, it destroyed our relationship."

I said, "I sat with your wife and spent almost three hours having her try to find all the blessings and the positives about you and your relationship. She initially had about 75 negative and 5 positive things. As a result of her imbalanced perception, she's been seeing another man for eight years that you didn't even know about."

There was a stunned silence, and then he blurted out, "My wife's been sleeping with somebody else? What am I supposed to do about *that?*"

People want to blame someone else when they don't understand their accountability for their own reality. Have you ever noticed that blame doesn't empower you? It can, in fact, be very disempowering, and it won't get you what you would truly love in life.

I said, "Look, whatever you repress in the equation of your relationship dynamic, somebody else comes to express."

If you're not having sex with your spouse, don't be surprised if they end up attracting what you fantasize about but don't do. As I spoke, he started to think I wasn't quite as terrible as he first thought, because I was now helping him see what was actually going on in his marriage.

I said, "If you want to keep your wife, listen to her. Find out what her values are, and learn how to effectively communicate in terms of them. Identify and own where you're repressing, disassociating, and blaming. Otherwise, she'll move on."

By her telling him she was ready to move on, he *woke up*. It was one of the best things that ever happened to their relationship. Before then, he'd been virtually saying, "I don't care about all that learning stuff. I don't want to grow; I just want to sit in my fantasy tradition that when you're married everything becomes set," but when he woke up, he suddenly wanted to learn about life and how to keep his marriage growing.

She temporarily moved out, and he came to The Breakthrough Experience. She'd been condemning him for years, and now he was becoming what she'd always hoped he would be. She started to appreciate and become attracted to him even more. Meanwhile, he began to empower himself. He was no longer in a state of *needing* her, but moved toward *loving* her. She began to be drawn to him, and saw more of her lover's downside. She then more fully Collapsed this fantasy man, balancing out her perceptions and appreciating her husband that much more. She'd been playing a self-righteous role, and he had been playing the other side. When he became more empowered like her and she became more humbled, they embraced more of their sides and met in the middle.

She moved back in with her husband, and they're still together. They made it through their crisis. If it wasn't for those events, they wouldn't have shifted. As he awakened to the truth of his relationship dynamic, he had nothing to forgive her for—her affair actually gave him his heart, his wife, and his *life* back, and that's exactly what they both truly wanted. It was the divine order working to create love. At the same time somebody tells me I destroyed their relationship, somebody else says I saved theirs, but the truth is that I just open hearts. I just help them get to their heart and find the truth of their inner love.

Soulmates

I often consult with people looking for the perfect relationship. They ask me, "How can I find my soulmate?"

The first thing I do is rule out the possibility that they may be living with a fantasy about a mate with only positives and no negatives. Since that one-sided mate doesn't exist, of course they won't be able to find them. And since they will attract their own disowned parts into their relationships, they will draw the opposite kind of mate into their lives. A mixture of their fantasy person combined with their reality person makes up the true soulmate, but they don't realize it.

The second thing I do is get them to tell me every single quality of their ideal partner and find out where these qualities already are in their lives. Only when they realize that it's already in their lives are they prepared to meet their soulmate. Life is funny. The moment you realize you already have everything you're looking for, the universe gives it to you. The instant you think you don't have something, it evades you further.

The greatest discovery in life is that no matter what you do, you're being supported and challenged simultaneously. The second greatest discovery is that nothing is missing; it's just in a form you haven't recognized. Widen your experience and broaden yourself, which is the value of experience, and see that it's all there just in a new form, and then watch yourself become a master of transformation.

When I was in college years ago, there were stacks of men's magazines in the dorm, and one day I picked up a *Oui* magazine and flipped through the pages. Something grabbed me, and it wasn't a breast, a pair of legs or anything like that. It was a picture of the most beautiful woman and a very handsome man standing with their arms around each other, both naked, and you could *tell* it was not just a pose; it was a picture of love. When I saw that picture, I projected my dream woman and myself onto it, and it somehow became real.

I carried that picture for 18 years, until my wife appeared. The gorgeous girl in the photo was just like her. Today, the picture has become real.

Do you have an inner image of "the one" that you compare everybody else to? The clearer, more balanced, more real, and whole that image is—and the more you love yourself (because it's really a reflection of your true self)—the more power you have in creating or attracting your special mate. And don't imagine that when you meet your soulmate it will be only roses, gondolas, and moonlight. Your soulmate will bring you the greatest experiences of pleasure and pain, the biggest supports and challenges of your life. That is true love.

Two people start out in a relationship with masks on, afraid they won't be loved for being themselves. But if you know that no matter what you've done or not done you're worthy of love, and if you see that everything you've done has served, then you're not afraid to take off the mask. You may not even wear one in the first place.

Everyone outside of you is a reflection and a part of you. Love *yourself* enough to love *them*. I've met so many people who put on facades and masks and try to convince themselves that they don't love the people they love, but I don't buy it for a second. I know better. There is nothing but love, and all else is illusion. The power to transform your life is in your heart. You only need the courage to open it.

Exercise

There are no victims in this world. We are all the cause and creators of our own perceptual experience. Until we acknowledge this fundamental truth, no true healing transformation or awakening can take place.

1. The next time someone does something that really pushes your buttons, instead of immediately reacting, stop! Give yourself one minute to consider, and think, *How do I do that, either identically or in my own form? How does it serve others that I behave in this way? How does it serve me that they're doing it now? What part did I play in making sure this happened?*

2. You'll probably be unable to think clearly in the heat of the moment, but that's okay; pausing for even a moment between trigger and response is progress. Go over the encounter in your mind later when you're alone, and find the hidden mirror.

The more you become accustomed to thinking in this way, the more you'll be able to do it in the moment. You'll be amazed at the effects on others—and on you—when you transcend a moment of judgment and blame.

Words of Wisdom and Power

*   *Happiness and sadness are the two sides of fulfillment.*
*   *I speak from my heart, and people listen.*
*   *If two people are exactly the same, one of them isn't necessary.*
*   *Put them on a pedestal, put them in the pit.*
*   *Love them for who they are, and they become who you love.*
*   *There is nothing but love, and all else is illusion.*

Chapter Seven

Divinity

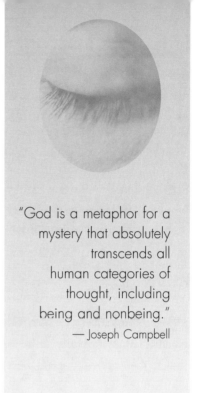

"God is a metaphor for a
mystery that absolutely
transcends all
human categories of
thought, including
being and nonbeing."
— Joseph Campbell

Imagine a galaxy with 700 billion stars just like our sun, moving in perfect order around its center. When those stars are on the side closest to the neighboring galaxy, it's like daylight to them; and when they're on the other side of their galaxy, it's like nighttime. But if we were to go into the middle of our galaxy, the very center of centers where nothing goes around in circles because it's the *center*, that's a point of rest. In some theologies, that center of centers has been called "God."

God has been conceived as the resting point, what the ancient Greeks called "the unmoving mover." There is movement all around, but the unmoving mover is the initiator of all motion. The true students of spirit and seekers of wisdom walk toward their own center of centers, where the unmoving mover is, into the galaxy of their own consciousness with its constellations of personas. They're not caught in the cycles of day and night, positive and negative, light and dark, but are willing to move more directly to the center of those dualities.

Like figure skaters who spin slowly when their arms are out-stretched and faster as they come closer to their center, the students' rate of spin and vibration also increases. They see the cycles of light and dark much faster, and as they approach wisdom, they also approach a point where they're at rest. They don't react to the changes around them, because for a moment they're the center that doesn't move.

Guru Nanak

The founder of the Sikh religion was a great teacher named Guru Nanak. This wise being dedicated his life to studying the world's religions. In his spiritual quest, he went to Israel and studied Judaism and Christianity, he journeyed to Mecca to study Mohammed's teachings, and he went to the Kaaba, a cubical building in the center of Mecca's big square.

On the eastern side of the Kaaba is a sacred stone, a meteorite set into the wall. Guru Nanak walked into the square and lay down on his back in meditation with his feet toward the sacred stone. The Muslims around him were deeply offended because the stone is a symbol of Allah, and the feet are considered unclean. They cried out in their language, "Blasphemy! Blasphemy! How dare you put your feet to the sacred stone?"

They pushed his feet away, but he just spun around and they were magically brought back to the stone. They kicked him, they dragged him out, they rolled him over and around and dragged him away, but nothing they did seemed to make the slightest difference. He kept his feet pointing to the stone.

Everyone was upset and screaming at him, and he finally asked them, "Brothers, why are you so upset?"

"Because the sacred stone represents God, and you don't put your feet in the direction of God. That is bad!"

He said, "If you can tell me where God is *not*, I will gladly put my feet there."

We're all hypocrites when we say we're spiritual but don't sit in a state of gratitude and grace for the magnificence of everything, just as it is. None of us are going to do that 24 hours a day, but if we're wise, we're honest enough with ourselves to acknowledge the times when we're not grateful, know that that's the journey, and humble ourselves to our sacred path of love.

Divinity is not some authoritarian personality from theological or religious teaching. The root of the word *divine* means "to shine," and as we shine, illuminate, and become brilliant, we approach divinity. To me, "God" stands for Grand Organized Design in the universe, or if you want to personify it, you can call it the Grand Organizing Designer. God is the source of what the physicist David Bohme called the "implicate order." We project onto the world our myth of how it should be, but the truth is an underlying order, and it's our job to discover it.

Divine order is like the puzzle game called Concentration. At first, we have no idea of the underlying order, but every time we join two pieces in a way that they match, we get a glimpse of what's hidden underneath, and the big picture suddenly falls into place. In our lives, we're picking up all the pieces we don't see divine order in, experiencing both sides, and integrating them until we see it—and once we know it exists, we start looking for it everywhere. The more we look for that order, the more we find it. It's like buying a new BMW and suddenly seeing BMWs everywhere. Divinity is virtually smacking us in the face, but we don't want to recognize it. We feel in dis-grace because we don't acknowledge it in ourselves and in every part of our lives.

Going to Heaven

Have you ever been approached by people who said, "I have to help you because I'm afraid your soul is going to rot in hell unless you're *saved*"?

I've asked many groups of fundamentalists to describe heaven for me, and they either turn their backs and walk away, or they say, "I don't know how to answer you; I'll have to ask my superiors," and of course *they* don't know either, but they've been living their lives as if they knew heaven.

I once spoke to 275 members of a Presbyterian church and asked them what heaven was. No two people in the audience had the same answer. They all belonged to the same religion, all thought they were going to different places in different ways, and all believed they shared the same belief.

Heaven is actually a state of being, and it has an infinite number of quantum levels. The way to expand to the next level is through gratitude. Heaven is a state of the heart when you feel grateful, and every time you're not grateful, that's hell. I don't disagree with the fundamentalists about going somewhere higher, but you don't do it in just your physical body. You are basically spiritual-material vibrations, and as you raise the frequency of your vibrations through love and gratitude, you attune to ever-higher spheres of that infinite heaven. And there's no end to it.

I've consulted with people for many years now, and I've seen that what they once thought of as chaos they eventually found the order in—if they were willing to look. There exists a hidden order behind any apparent chaos, but most people don't understand it. We do not perceive divinity in duality, for in duality we have only lopsided illusions about it. Divinity is the synthesis, the wholeness, that is conceived in the eternal present, that presence we feel when we've united or merged some pairs of opposites living in duality. Presence is the closest experience we have to divinity.

The Law of Conservation is inviolable. You are made out of the same energy and matter as the whole universe. Therefore, *you* won't violate this law either. That's why the will of God is equilibrium, why there is nothing but love, and all else is illusion. No matter what you perceive, underneath your senses it's all balanced and present.

The Great Artist

Some people ask why we have to bring God or Divine Intelligence into it at all. They believe that if we can't see something, it's safer or even somehow *wiser* to assume it doesn't exist. No scientist on Earth has ever seen an atom or a radio wave, and nobody knows what electricity is. Physicists find it nearly impossible to write an equation describing even something as elementary as the stretching of a rubber band. Yet no one doubts that these things exist.

Scientists now estimate that 3.9 billion years ago, living microorganisms and cells existed on Earth. Even that long ago, those cells were so magnificently designed that it boggles the minds of the greatest physiologists today to understand how they functioned. How is it that something so evolved, with so much intelligence and order, could have preceded us when we so self-righteously think of *ourselves* as the highest form of intelligence and order? To insist that an unbelievably complex cell is the result of some random thermal event is the height of folly. With all of our intelligence, the greatest human mind in history is incapable of running a single cell. You could link Isaac Newton, Plato, Albert Einstein, and Stephen Hawking together and they still couldn't do it—they couldn't even approach it.

People talk about admiring the CEO of a major corporation with 50,000 employees, but I see a human body and say, "Now *that's* management!" They look at a painting or a sculpture and say, "That artist is a genius," but the greatest work of art ever created is like a child's mud pie or finger painting compared to the genius and artistry of a human being, the life that fills it, and the Divine Artist who created it.

Because we're surrounded by life and divinity, we take it all for granted, like a fish unaware of the water it lives in. Life truly is a miracle, and miracles don't happen by chance alone but by laws and intelligence. That intelligence has set in place the principles that govern life. The Deity doesn't watch over and judge us any more than It personally directs the movement of every molecule in every cell of every being. The universe is a big place, and it works like any big organization, by hierarchy and delegation. God is too busy to punish anyone; He just sets up the dynamics of evolution through universal laws and stands back emanating divine love. In that divine order, life and death are in perfect balance, conserved throughout time and space.

Everyone knows about the 168 people killed in the Oklahoma City bombing, but most do not realize what *didn't* happen. The suicide, homicide, disease, and accidental death rates in that city dropped, and the death rate came out the same as most every other month. All that changed was the *form* of death. Those figures were reported in *USA Today* and the *Dallas Star,* but anyone who didn't understand universal laws would think it was just a coincidence.

When an earthquake struck Oakland, California, and three dozen people died in the freeway collapse, there were too many casualties for one hospital, so they were distributed between several in the area. Nine months later, the births in those hospitals jumped by the same three dozen over the normal rate. That, too, went unnoticed.

A young man named Martin Bryant shot 35 people in Australia, many of them children. As a direct result of that shooting, Australia's national gun laws were changed and hundreds of thousands of weapons were turned in, possibly saving many lives for years to come. The entire country stopped for a moment of prayer that no religion on Earth could have accomplished—turning people's minds to thoughts of immortal spirit and physical mortality. Parents all around that part of the world, when they heard about it, probably held their children close that night and thought, *Thank you for being alive. I'm grateful I still have you.* The life and the love were conserved.

There Are No Victims

"You might ask, 'How can I know if something is God's will?'
My answer is, 'If it were not God's will, it wouldn't exist
even for an instant; so if something happens, it must be His will.
If you truly enjoyed God's will, you would feel exactly as
though you were in the kingdom of heaven, whatever
happened to you or didn't happen to you.'"
— Meister Eckhart

Many people ask, "If there is a God, why does he let so many terrible things happen, like battered women, illness, and war? What about all the innocent victims?"

Domestic violence is more than just a touchy subject today; it's a way of life for the millions of women who feel trapped and frightened by it. Many battered spouses have attended The Breakthrough Experience, women who've been beaten up in one relationship after another. But first appearances are often deceiving. Repetitive violence is not the "fault" of the "abuser"; these so-called victims batter themselves inside, put themselves down, and think they're worthless. They commonly receive an overly gentle and elevating support from others that compensates and balances, and they sometimes become martyrs for the purpose of this support. They minimize themselves and don't acknowledge that they're magnificent or of value to the world, and they keep associating with and drawing in men who treat them that way.

When I take them through The Quantum Collapse Process and help them see why they're beating themselves up inside and how their unappreciated qualities served them and other people, they raise their self-worth. When they go home, without even *saying* anything, their family or relationship changes. They either move on and no longer get caught in those cycles, or the person they're with spontaneously stops beating them.

This is not meant to excuse violent actions or say that they're good, but the moment you honor yourself and stop thinking you're worthless, so will your partner. There's a *dynamic* going on; it's not a violent villain and an innocent victim—it's a team playing out a balancing duality. When you understand what's actually happening, you see that it's perfectly ordered, with two people teaching each other how to grow in self-worth and love.

It's unwise to separate cause and effect, because the minute you do, you make yourself a victim. As long as you blame someone else for what's happening to you, you will be a victim, disempowered, and you will not find a solution. You have to acknowledge your own cause and effect to enlighten and awaken your own reality. I haven't seen anyone liberate themselves, nor seen anyone open their heart or become empowered, by blaming and playing the victim. No liberation is complete until you realize that your perceptions are your own cause, and it's up to you to empower yourself. The second you understand that you're playing a role that attracted those forces, you have the power to transform that reality. You *are* the author of your own life.

I Am Worthy of Love

A number of years ago, I had the opportunity to talk with a gentleman in a San Francisco hospital who was dying of AIDS. The doctors gave him just a couple of weeks to live. When I came into his room, he was emaciated, covered with sores, leaning over in bed, and propped up with pillows. I sat down next to him and grabbed his hands and wouldn't let go.

I'd never met the man until that moment, but I just held his hands and looked him straight in the eye and said, "No matter what you've done or not done, you're worthy of love. No matter what you've done or not done, you're worthy of love." I had him repeat it over and over again until it finally penetrated his heart and he started to cry. He leaned over into my lap, and I put my hands on his back and kept saying, "No matter what you've done, you're worthy of love," while he cried and cried and cried.

He finally lifted up his head a little bit and looked at me and said, "That's the first time in my entire life I've ever thought that. That's the first time I've ever given myself permission to love myself."

In spite of the dire prognosis, that man lived almost two more years.

AIDS is said to be an autoimmune disease, but I believe that it results from the body turning against itself partly because the mind has turned against itself. Most diseases have an underlying emotional basis; I have yet to find one that doesn't. Twenty-nine years ago, medical journals listed a handful of recognized psychosomatic illnesses. Today that list numbers more than 100, and in the next ten years, it will probably be many hundreds.

Disease and illness are the signs and symptoms that the body uses to reveal to us where we're not loving. This divinely created system makes sure we get the message, and wakes us up to the truth that nothing in ourselves or the world is unworthy of love.

Most headaches are a result of ignoring the soul's inner guidance and wisdom. They represent a conflict between the emotional effect of the senses and the clarity of the inner voice. Try this the next time you have one: Stop and become present with silence. Allow yourself to hear the message of your inner voice and follow its guidance, and

THE BREAKTHROUGH EXPERIENCE

watch your headache subside. It's truly astonishing.

I've worked with terminal cancer patients who had spontaneous remissions, and in each case, some form of love and gratitude came into their lives and shifted them. A spiritual experience transformed their illness. Even watching a movie about love has been shown to increase the levels of immunoglobulin A in the saliva, the body's first line of immunological defense. We get ill to teach us to love. It's not a punishment or a mistake. It's a gift.

Every symptom and sign in your physical body is designed to reveal to you what you're lying about. Our emotions are lies. Our elation and depression are lies. Emotions are the result of lopsided perceptions. They become electrical charges that affect your physiology, turning on and off cells, tissues, and organs. Illness is your body's way of telling you that you're lying about life. You're seeing what you think is attractive and repulsive instead of what is lovingly magnificent. So just in case there's a fragment somewhere in your life that for some reason you think is difficult to love, just know that that's an illusion. You *are* worthy of love. Say the following words of power: *No matter what I've done or not done, I am worthy of love.* When every single cell of your body vibrates with these words, so will you, and so will your world.

Thank You for My Life

There is a meaning behind all events, and wisdom is finding and saying "thank you" for your meaningful life. If you look wisely, everything in your life is perfect exactly as it is; and anything you can't find meaning in, you will be uncertain and ungrateful for. In that state, you don't see the magnificence of your world and think that if you somehow leave this place, life will be better somewhere else. According to one survey, 97 percent of Americans are looking for something meaningful after they depart from this wonderful planet instead of loving the people on it now.

Some people say, "Yeah, I know, but there are certain things in life that I couldn't love. What about this and this, and my God, what about this?" I have yet to find anything on this planet that wasn't serving someone in some way.

I worked with a woman in Canada who was raped when she was 18 years old. She was angry and bitter about the event, but she ended up becoming a gynecologist who specialized in women who had been raped. She *loved* her work. She felt fulfilled and worthwhile and became a leader in her field, renowned for her skills and expertise.

When she came to The Breakthrough Experience program, I had her Collapse her rapist and find the magnificence of that event in her life. Her whole career arose from that experience, but she had never thanked the man until that day. She listed the positives and negatives and balanced them out, and found where she had committed all the components of rape in her own form. She saw where people perceived that she had violated their privacy, dominated them psychologically, made them do things they didn't want to do—it was basically her whole life; she did it every day. I had her identify her mirroring reflection and own whatever she saw in the rapist.

I then asked her, "Who in this room reminds you of the rapist?"

She looked around the room and picked a guy sitting in the corner, and out of that whole group, she chose the one who had actually been accused of rape. She sat with him and told him how he had helped her life, and she thanked him.

At the end of their exchange, he said, "I just want to thank you for setting me free, because I've been in a prison ever since that day."

The whole room was in tears, with chills up their spines at the magnificence of the universe that brought these two together. When I tell that story, people who have never gotten past their own rape often stand up, react, or walk out, saying, "That man is out of his mind." I encourage you stick it out and find the blessings, because otherwise it will run your life. And equilibrating your perceptions sets you free.

If we label the rapist "evil" and call the woman "a victim," we help them both become stuck. We put him in jail, but we put her in prison, too. We support her and tell her she's an innocent victim, and she stays in her self-imposed prison the rest of her life. The people in this story both ended up becoming quite extraordinary individuals *because of*—not in spite of—their experiences.

You can live in the past and never get on with the future, and I assure you that anything you don't love about your past will affect your future. Why would you want to give someone you despise the power to run your life? Why would the Jewish people want to give Hitler the power to run their lives for more than 50 years? That reveals an unwillingness to probe deeper into the equilibrating and compensating laws of the universe. Have you ever met anyone who condemned their first wife or husband and then went out and found another just like them?

Anything you don't love about a past relationship of any kind you bring right into your next one; you keep dealing with it because it's not about them, it's about you. Love yourself enough to love them, and set both of you free.

Everything Serves

Bruce Lee became the world's greatest martial artist because as a young man he was badly beaten in the streets of Hong Kong and swore he wouldn't let it happen again. Director Martin Scorsese had asthma as a child and was kept in an attic room where he watched the world go by through a tiny window, like a camera lens, and imagined stories about the people below. Nelson Mandela used his 28 years in prison to develop his wisdom and understanding, becoming a symbol for freedom and racial harmony and emerging as the leader of his entire nation.

I've worked with hundreds of people who lost a loved one and found that that was the exact moment when their emotional walls were broken down. That was when they opened their hearts to those around them, when their spirituality and awareness of an afterlife or eternal spirit was birthed, when they found a real purpose in being alive. Even life and death are in perfect balance, and in times of adversity, we go within to find a deeper sense of life.

Everything has two sides, and you can never have one without the other. It's not one side now and the other maybe sometime in the future; they're simultaneous. Don't wait to get old to finally understand this. Awaken to the wisdom of the ages without the aging process. Honor the truth of equilibration.

Benefit and drawback, the positive and the negative, are always perfectly balanced. The further down and out you've been, the further up and in you can go. The early lives of the great masters were characterized by challenge and hardship. That's where they unveiled their power to achieve what they did.

"If you ever wake up without a problem, you better get down on your knees and pray for one, because otherwise you just died."
— Norman Vincent Peale

Don't complain about your lot. Instead, ask yourself, "How does my illness serve? What is the hidden benefit to my fear or confusion or lack of money?" and don't stop until you're thankful for it.

Does it make you slow down, seek healing, remind you of your mortality and stop taking life for granted, return to basics and take responsibility for your life? Does it help you dig inside and find courage, be grateful for small things, humble you, attract help and support, motivate you to get creative and get real? I promise you that the blessing is there, but you must be willing to look for it.

Anything you perceive as life-threatening or destroying is also life-giving and creating, if you only have the wisdom to look for it. Find that balance in your world, and enter into a freedom that few people ever experience, the liberty of an inspiring and trusting life.

Big Gratitude

A gentleman came in for a consultation and said in a rushed and anxious voice, "I'm really overweight, and I've just got to get rid of it. If I could just change this one thing, my life would be so much better."

So I asked him, "How is it serving you?"

At first he refused to believe that it served him in any way at all, but eventually he came up with 89 benefits to being overweight. He received attention when he walked into a room, women were drawn to him because they thought he was vulnerable and safe, and it gave him an excuse to put off writing the book on healing that he didn't feel ready to write. We came up with blessing after blessing, and after about two hours, he discovered how it unconsciously served him.

If you can see that everything in your life serves you, that no matter what you've done or not done it's moving you forward, you suddenly see your own perfection and your heart opens—to yourself.

There is a widespread, temporary social infatuation with a particular physical type, and I've worked with so many people who beat themselves up and block their genius because they don't match it. Some beautiful women gained weight because they couldn't take the constant pressure of male attention and female envy, and it was easier to just opt out of the game. One woman used her weight to stay faithful to her husband; she didn't trust herself to be attractive and still say no to other men. Some people used it to avoid or attract sex, attention, or responsibility. Some were afraid to live their dreams, so they kept their metabolic rate low to avoid having energy, and the responsibility that came with it. I've consulted with several beautiful women who used weight as a screening device. They were sick of men being attracted to their physical self and ignoring their inner beauty, and their weight automatically preselected males who were able to look deeper and see them for who they really were. They were like the maidens in a fairy tale, under an enchantment that only the eyes of a true heart could penetrate. They were looking for "the one," and they traded their appearance for love.

It was never a mistake, just the best strategy they could come up with at the time to serve some higher value or goal. Their motives were actually quite noble. Once we found their motives, we were able to come up with different strategies to achieve the same result. These women stopped despising themselves and got on with their lives, and their weight often returned to what was normal for them.

It's our job to look beyond our illusions or myths and find the underlying truth. When we become humbled to the Intelligence greater than ourselves, we get beyond ourselves and open the doorway to expansion. But the second we project onto the world what we think it's supposed to be rather than acknowledging what it is, we automatically hold ourselves back.

Although there's nothing inherently wrong with not recognizing the beauty of life, the true living spiritual experience occurs when we acknowledge God's magnificence and grace in presence, love, and gratitude. That's a holy communion in its purest nature, and it *is* attainable. We're not going to remain in grace, but we have the ability to experience it and get a glimpse of what's possible. The vitality and power that surge from recognizing it won't allow us to remain unchanged. We'll be transformed into a new person in life. That is the rebirthing process; which is how we become truly reborn, because we realize that there is a magnificent and hidden order. That's what my whole work is about.

Grasping this is a human possibility. There's an Intelligence that permeates you, and it is vast. That Intelligence is available to you through inspiration and intuition, to guide and direct your life. It has the power to organize the cell, and to organize all life-forms. It has the power to organize *you*.

The Myth of Forgiveness

Have you ever noticed that anything you say "I forgive you" for, you keep attracting into your life; and anything you say "I'm sorry" for, you keep doing? Why? Because anything you apologize for or forgive, you're judging as not being a part of divine order, and you'll keep experiencing it until you understand how it's exactly that. Anything you feel guilty about, you repeat; and anything you forgive, you keep attracting into your life.

Forgiveness is a self-righteous illusion that makes someone bad or wrong and then presumes to judge and pardon. Apology is judging yourself, and both are guaranteed to perpetuate whatever you judge. The only thing that transcends this dynamic is love.

People ask me, "Does that mean that if you run into somebody, you don't have to say you're sorry?"

Yes, it does. There are far more creative ways of dealing with such things. I bumped into a man in a hurry at a restaurant recently who said apologetically, "Oh, excuse me," but I immediately turned to him and said, "Hi, I'm Dr. Demartini. We must have been attracted to each other for a reason. What's your name?" and put my hand out to exchange a handshake.

I started a conversation, made an interesting acquaintance, and almost enrolled him in my seminar that weekend. Instead of thinking that it was a mistake, feeling guilty, apologizing, and running that whole illusion, why not see it as some kind of synchronicity? There are no mistakes in a divinely ordered universe. Why play into the illusion by apologizing for and forgiving divine order? Go beyond forgiveness, find the order, and be present with whatever happens. Of course you may be thinking that this isn't proper social etiquette, but neither is buying into or promoting unnecessary fear and guilt and helping people add to their already overloaded emotional baggage.

There are millions if not *billions* of people in the world talking about forgiveness. There exists a hierarchy of emotional responses in life. Fear and guilt are at the bottom of the ladder; above them are faith, acceptance, and forgiveness; and at the top is the present truth of love, appreciation, and wisdom. Forgiveness is a stage on the path, but once you see that everything serves and there is nothing to forgive, it becomes another myth. The truth requires no forgiveness.

In my first book, *Count Your Blessings,* I said that forgiveness is a self-righteous illusion. When I presented The Breakthrough Experience to a Pentecostal Christian group and spoke to the ministers afterwards, they questioned me about that statement. At first they argued with me, but once I explained what I meant, they calmed down and agreed.

Because caring is speaking in terms of others' values, I said to them, "I say that forgiveness is a self-righteous illusion because you're assuming that God isn't present in that experience. Anytime you deny the presence of the divine order of God, the lopsided 'devil' rules your life. If you're truly in Christ-consciousness, you don't judge; you simply love. Thine enemy is thyself. Remove the beam from your own eye before you attempt to take the mote from another's."

The ministers nodded in agreement and said, "In that context, that's a Christian teaching!"

Then I added, "And this means *anything.*"

They all thought a moment before saying, "That's disturbing, even frightening, but it seems to be true."

It's a paradox, isn't it? It means that every time we judge anything and don't see its magnificence, we're denying God. That's hard for some ministers to own because they're caught in their own self-imposed dilemma. They're trying to say, "He's in everything but *that*. God is missing there," but I say, "Where is God *not?*"

The only real meaning of forgiveness to me is, "Thank you *for giving* me this experience," whatever it may be. If you can say that, you're no longer fearful or a victim. I call it *true transcendent forgiveness*. When most people use the term, they mean, "I forgive you, but don't ever do it again." And what that really means is, "I still have a button on this. I judge you, and I'm righteous enough to put you down and humble you over it."

To me, that's incomplete and conditional love. It implies guilt and is but a stepping-stone along the way to the truth of love. When everything else has been tried and experienced, then comes love. To kneel down at the side of your bed just like a little child and count your blessings is wisdom. When you humble yourself enough to kneel down and give thanks, you become illuminated. I don't mean it in the sense of groveling or feeling small, I mean humbling yourself until you become receptive to the great permeating Intelligence that governs this living universe.

Even though some deny the existence of divinity and say that life is the result of chance and random thermal motions, subject to entropy and dissolution and without meaning, I say that there's a vastly greater Intelligence than the one that declares such a futile message. My message is for you to look inside and commune with that Intelligence daily.

Did you know that if every night at bedtime you say "thank you" for what you've experienced during the day, that great Intelligence would resonate with you and speak clearly through to your heart? If every morning before you get out of bed you stop and think of what you're grateful for—your children, spouse, life, or opportunities—that Voice will speak to you. Every time you don't listen to the intuition and inspiration of your soul, you break down; and every time you listen to it, you awaken your genius.

Infinite Intelligence

The Milky Way galaxy alone contains some 700 billion stars just like our own sun. There are billions of galaxies in one galaxy cluster, and billions of galaxy clusters in one super-cluster. These are unbelievably vast proportions, but those stars, galaxies, clusters, and super-clusters are all moving toward a common objective, some great attractor. An Intelligence governs their motion and guides them along their paths; great minds throughout the centuries who were not atheistic or emotionally charged acknowledged this to be true.

I wonder what would happen if we started to listen to that Intelligence, if we obeyed and followed its guidance? A genius is one who follows the light of their soul and obeys. We must humble ourselves to this Intelligence if we ever want to get beyond ourselves. The moment we humble ourselves to that infinite Intelligence, we begin to share in it. We acknowledge ourselves as part of it, and we start to receive the guidance and inspiration that will take us where we're destined to go, and where we would most love to be.

Exercise

You're constantly being told stories about life here on Earth by newspapers, radio, television, books, and friends—and even your own thoughts. Those stories are almost invariably polarized to one side or the other, positively or negatively, because mass-media consciousness often thrives among the extremes labeled "good" and "evil."

1. The next time you hear, see, or read a story that pushes your buttons one way or the other, stop and look for the other side. Whether positive or negative, look for the nonlocally connected event that balances it in the other direction.

2. Ask how this event serves the world and the people involved. Ask yourself, *How is God revealed in this event?* and don't stop until you see it.

My friend entered the elevator of his building in New York City one morning, just after a big earthquake in Turkey had killed hundreds of people. The heavily televised story was on his mind, so he said to the elderly elevator man, "Isn't it terrible what's happening in Turkey? All those poor people!" The elevator operator replied, "You know, I don't question God's work anymore." He wasn't indifferent or callous; he just had such wisdom and certainty of Divinity that he went straight to the heart of that event.

Exercise your wisdom. Train yourself to instantly equilibrate emotions on a global scale, and the more you do, the more certain you will become about the governing Intelligence that orders life on Earth.

Words of Wisdom and Power

- *Where is God* not?
- *Gratitude is heaven, ingratitude is hell.*
- *Everything serves, including me.*
- *Nothing is missing; it just changes form.*
- *There are no victims, just lessons in love.*
- *Forgiveness is a passing milestone on the path of love and truth.*

Chapter Eight

Genius

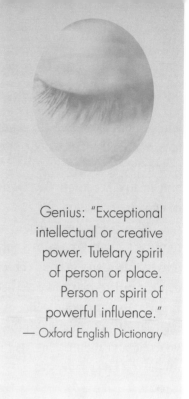

Genius: "Exceptional
intellectual or creative
power. Tutelary spirit
of person or place.
Person or spirit of
powerful influence."
— Oxford English Dictionary

I was blessed when I was very young to meet a great teacher who had extremely powerful certainty. His certainty was so profound that he saw the possibilities in me and everyone else around him. He saw our genius. His certainty was so great that my questions and doubts were overridden, and for a timeless period, I saw myself as he saw me. He helped awaken my inner vision, and for that I remain humble and grateful.

I believe we have a mortal self and an immortal self, a part of us that's run by the outer world and a part that's called from the inner world. To the degree that we listen to the inner voice and vision rather than the outer, we awaken our immortal genius and inspiration.

The word *genius* comes from the Latin root meaning "guardian spirit," and that's exactly what great teachers and immortal thinkers are: creative, guardian spirits who shine light on what seems dark to others. Our own soul is the ultimate guardian spirit, and a genius is one who listens to their soul and obeys.

That state where we acknowledge the immortal and the infinite tends to birth the greatest genius. Masterpieces of art, music, litera-ture, and mathematics pour through us in an inspired fashion. We're infinitely attuned; and we can see, feel, or hear the bigger design, holistically. We know that we're a small but complete part of some-thing vast.

What if you knew that every event in your life was guiding you to the acknowledgment of your infinity, the holographic piece of the universe that sits inside each of us? What if every heartbeat, every cellular pulse, every muscle and tendon of your body, every micro-filament within your cells, was all doing everything it could to reawaken you to that possibility? What would happen if you silenced yourself and didn't deny it, but simply allowed it to shine? What might you be capable of?

Angelic Music

I'm sure you've met people who are extraordinary and wondered to yourself, *How did they do that? How did they accomplish so much?* I remember sitting in the makeup room of a Dallas television show, being prepared for the cameras next to a lovely little girl who was also getting her makeup done. I started a conversation.

"Are you going on the show?"

She answered in a tiny, breathy voice, "Yes."

"And what are you going to do?"

"I'm going to play the violin."

I said, "Oh, that's wonderful," but I saw only a little girl. I wasn't acknowledging the potential of her genius, and inside I thought, *She's going to try playing her violin on TV. How sweet.*

On the makeup-room monitor, I watched her go out onto the set, and by the time I tiptoed into the wings, she was sitting in the chair about to be interviewed. The co-hosts talked to her as if she was just a sweet young child; they had no idea who she really was inside. Then she stood up and put the violin under her chin, closed her eyes, and began to play.

With tears flowing down her cheeks, that little girl went off into some extraordinary realm in an impossible, inexplicable masterpiece of music. I thought, *How could that possibly be? It's inconceivable that she should be a master of the violin; she's just a child.*

When she finished, she opened up her twinkling little eyes. The hosts' makeup was running down their faces, and the camera operators were disoriented. They were still with her music, and they were blown away, just as I was.

I was to be interviewed next about my book, *Count Your Blessings,* and the power of genius, so the timing was perfect. I said to the hosts, "That was it. That's my message right there. She just got off the stage. She is worth counting our blessings for."

The lady interviewer's facade was gone, her partner's mask was gone, the camera operators' facades were gone, all masks were swept away by an experience of the divinity of infinity. The purity of the essence, the ascension of the human spirit, was expressed in that harmonious moment. That tiny violinist was a master at work, a genius expressed. Her creativity was born on the spot. It was whole and complete.

Imagine if you allowed yourself the honor of saying, "I'm worth it. I discipline and master those skills I'm destined to express," whatever they might be. In the little girl's case, it happened to be music; with you, it may be anything on Earth, but there is within you a talent tapped to your infinity. It is divinely expressible, unique, creative, and when others see it come out of you, they will recognize it as true genius. It's your destiny. You have a yearning and a knowing inside every one of your cells that is linked to your infinite nature.

The Seven Levels of Consciousness

Genius is not a matter of intellect; it is a result of listening to and acting upon the messages of your soul. Genius is actually a function of love, because the more love you have, the more you can raise your frequency and tune in to those inspiring messages. You have the option to repress or express your genius, and your perceptions determine which one you will choose. Imagine that there are seven levels of consciousness relating to the seven levels of brain evolution and verbal expression:

Verbal Expression	Level of Consciousness	Perception Ratio	Brain Evolution	Stage of Evolvement	Life Results
Love to	Self-actualization	(1-1)	Corpus Callosum	Spiritual Human	*Break Through* Inspiration
Choose to	Self-fulfillment	(2-1)	Cerebral Cortex	Human Mammal	
Desire to	Self-esteem	(3-1)	Limbic Brain	Mammalian	
Want to	Social	(4-1)	Basal Ganglia	Reptilian-Apes	*Break Even*
Need to	Security	(5-1)	Brain Stem	Amphibian	
Ought to	Survival	(6-1)	Spinal Cord	Pre-amphibian	
Have to	Suicide	(7-1)	Neuron	Unicellular	*Break Down* Desperation

The chart above represents the possible scale of emotional expression. The bottom of the scale represents a low-frequency state, involving imbalance; and desperation is the primary motivating force. The top of the scale represents a high-frequency state, involving balance; and inspiration is the primary motivating force. The more balanced your perceptions, the higher you rise. At the top of the scale, you acknowledge that you're more than just an individual; you're connected to and perfectly reflect the universal whole.

The third column, the perception ratio, compares negatives to positives. For example, the 7-1 ratio at the bottom of the chart indicates that you see something as having seven times more negatives than positives, and you *have to* get away from it. If you perceive seven times as many positives as negatives, you *have to* have it. If the ratio is 6-1, you feel you should or *ought to* have or get away from it; 5-1 means you *need to* have it or get away from it, and so on up the chart.

We all jump up and down the scale at different times and in different areas of our lives. Mastery in any area of life simply means finding the balance and not being ruled by emotions. All things *are* balanced, so why not know this and begin to look for the equilibrium? In that state, there's no perception of gain or loss; you're poised, and have mastery over whatever you do.

Many people live in the desperate have-to level: "I *have to* go to work; I *have to* get them back in my life." They think that an oppressive social force outside of themselves is forcing them to do something, and they're disassociated from their own inner power. Here at the bottom of the hierarchy, there is no choice; they're compelled to avoid and seek, and they spend every day doing things they think they *have to* do. If you're not doing what you love and loving what you do, don't expect to manifest your full genius.

At the ought-to level, life consists of, "I *should* do this. I *ought* to go there." Authority is still outside the self, but not as strong.

Most people live between the need and want levels, "I *need* this, but I *want* that." They don't manifest their dreams or genius because they don't listen to their inspirations and act on them. More than 90 percent of Americans depend on Social Security when they retire, and more than 60 percent of them also rely on family members. Most live for immediate gratification without long-term vision, listening to their senses and not their soul.

Until you get past the want-to level, there is little free will or choice. But with each successive level, there is an increase of inner self-motivation and a decrease in outer compulsion. At the desire-to level, you start acknowledging a dream; and at the choose-to level,

THE BREAKTHROUGH EXPERIENCE

you begin realizing that you can make it happen. At the love-to level, you know it's your destiny and nothing will stop you. Here, you break through to a new and more inspired level of being.

Great geniuses are willing to pay the price. They're willing to make sacrifices for their dreams. Instead of partying with their friends, they spend hours practicing, studying, and preparing. They give up pleasure and entertainment and face their fears and doubts. They do whatever it takes. There's nothing wrong with that, because pain and pleasure always come together in a pair.

I fly a lot, and I frequently have people sitting next to me saying things such as, "Oh, God, I hate flying. It's so crowded, and I hate waiting in line. It's so tiring, and I can't sleep in these damn chairs, and jet lag is a nightmare for me. I can't stand the food. It's so bumpy and I get so scared." They talk constantly about how terrible it is. That's 7-1 thinking; it's desperate, and it sabotages genius.

I have a totally different reality about flying. I think of it as my private plane with my chauffeurs up front; a large staff to take care of me; multiple bedrooms, bathrooms, and kitchens; and a big social gathering to interact with. I have a button to press for anything I want, a private computer and telephone system, and a personal movie theater. I can stand up front and sell books and products to a captive audience, I can give seminars or read poetry or do anything I like, and I'm getting paid to fly. Yes, there is a balance of excessive radiation, waiting in lines, and all the rest of the challenges that come with flying, but because I see that all is balanced, I've become grateful and have transformed the flying experience into something I love.

It's all about framing, and all it takes is asking certain quality questions: How does flying help me fulfill my mission? How does taking out the trash help me fulfill my mission? How does shaving or bathing help me fulfill my mission? When you ask these kinds of questions, then link them over and over again until you can say, "Thank God I get to do that," suddenly it's all fuel instead of baggage. That's 1-1 thinking, the kind that helps you become inspired.

The story you tell yourself about your life is what your life becomes.

Fair Exchange

Every level or stage contains the exact lessons you need to take you to the next level. When you try to rescue people whom you perceive as being in the desperation levels, you rob them of the life experiences they need to grow. They have the capacity to change their attitudes and transform their lives, but they may momentarily be denying their own powers.

We are two-sided, whole beings. Anyone who is expressing depression and inferiority is also repressing elation and superiority. If you try to rescue the self-wrongeous side, you'll end up being bitten by the self-righteous side when it finally shows itself. That's not ingratitude; that's the universe teaching you not to spend your life and resources rescuing and fixing what is already in perfect equilibrium.

Last year an old friend called to ask, "Can you loan me some money?" and I said, "No, I won't."

"But why? You've got plenty."

"I know, and the reason I do is because I know how to manage it. I don't give money to people who don't know how, because if I do, we both say good-bye to our money. They become dependent, and I get a lesson in economics."

"I will not give money to any cause that does not ensure dignity, accountability, productivity, and responsibility to the recipients."
— Nelson Rockefeller

My friend got upset and slammed the phone down, but she went out and learned how to be responsible. She organized herself, got two jobs, and saved some money. A few months later, she came to me and said, "Thank you for not rescuing me."

Her father had rescued her financially for years. When he died, the inheritance took care of her, and she had never stood on her own two feet. Her brother was the balance in the family dynamic; he left home early to become independent. He was the other side; that's the magnificence. If I had rescued her, I'd be perpetuating the same dynamic her dad had created. When there was no more money and nobody to rescue her, she became accountable and started saving and valuing wealth.

That lady stopped asking who could help her and started asking how she could help herself. Once she was willing to ask the question, she got the answer. The quality of your life is determined by the quality of the questions you ask. So don't think, *What do I have to do today?* or *What do I need?* Ask yourself, *What would I love to do today? What would I love to do with my life?* Ask a different question and get a different life, because the way you talk to yourself creates your reality.

The Seven Levels of the Brain

As stated earlier in this chapter, there are seven levels to the brain, from the most primitive neuron to the most evolved corpus callosum. A neuron functions in a manner that is all or none, on or off, white or black, good or evil, similar to how fundamentalists function in their respective areas of life. Their minds can't comprehend gray; they can only perceive white or black. That's why if you say something isn't bad, fundamentalists will hear you say that it's good. They're all-or-none people, and to them, anything that isn't good has to be bad.

The corpus callosum is the most evolved development of the brain. It joins the brain's left and right hemispheres and literally has trillions of neurological connections. It functions more like a universalist, who has more choices and greater freedom and love.

The seven levels of the brain retrace the seven levels of evolutionary consciousness. The more balanced your perceptions, the higher you go in brain evolution and the more powerful and insightful your mind becomes. The more imbalanced your perceptions, the lower you go in brain evolution and the less powerful and insightful your mind becomes.

We have the capacity to rewire and evolve our own neural circuitry. Thought expresses itself through conducting neural pathways. Nerves are surrounded by lipid myelin sheaths that increase their conductivity. The more primitive the nerve, the thicker its myelin and the faster it conducts. That's why when you get stressed, you find yourself behaving in a primitive or instinctive manner, because before you even have time to think, the more primitive nerve pathways take over and elicit a reaction. But nerve use increases myelin, so the more you train yourself to find balance and see order, the thicker and faster the more evolved pathways become. At the same time, the old neural pathways atrophy if they're not used, so they have less and less power over you. It's a two-way benefit that raises your level of consciousness.

You grow from *impulse,* where you simply react unconsciously to the world; to *instinct*, where you're ruled by your emotions; to *intellect*, where the mind starts to have some awareness of, and influence on, your destiny. In all of those states, the heart is relatively closed and cannot direct your life. When the heart opens a little, you start to have *intuition*; and when it opens even further, you get *inspiration.* Inspiration involves messages, visions, and feelings that show you why you're here. When the heart is completely open, it can receive divine *revelation*; and when you receive that, you cannot help but have a profound effect on the world. You *will* make a difference here simply by being.

We were created to be geniuses. We were designed to have clair-voyance, clairaudience, and clairsentience—to have photographic and audiographic minds that are present. When we clear the static of emotions or their underlying imbalanced perceptions, that's exactly what we have.

Anything you lie about distracts you, keeps you from being pres-ent, and dissipates your power. If you allow yourself to get elated, you force yourself into depression, and the higher you go, the lower you go. On a biochemical level, as long as your elation releases endorphins, your depression will release pain substances; they come together. If you're willing to give up the high and become centered, you won't have to go through the low.

Depression medication is a multibillion-dollar industry because people don't realize how much power they have over their own emo-tional swings. Instead of continuing the elation-depression cycle, there is an alternative. Realize that crisis is blessing, that terrible is terrific; and reach a point where positive and negative are synthesized into a present, centered wholeness. When you stop living in and for the imbalanced emotions, you open the door to genius.

Living Genius

I've appeared on many platforms in the last 25 years, and there has been only one place in all that time where I've truly been too humbled to speak. It was in a class taught by Marilyn Wilhelm, an extraordinary teacher who taught ordinary children between the ages of two and thirteen, from all over the world. Her certainty exceeded all doubts about their extraordinary and ingenious potential because she taught them as if they already were geniuses, and that's exactly what they became.

I had come to speak to her class of eight-year-olds. When I asked if there were any questions, a Japanese boy raised his hand and said, "Dr. Demartini, I have a question. I would like to know the modus operandi of how endorphins work in the cerebral hemispheres of the brain."

I was amazed. I had the answer—that wasn't the problem—but I wasn't expecting that type of a question from such a young child. I was stuck in a different paradigm, and I realized from that moment on that I was no longer going to teach eight-year-olds as children; I was going to teach them as immortal *souls* inhabiting the earth. They may have little bodies, but they have miraculous and possibly ancient minds. The wisdom is in them, and it's in us. All we must do is recognize it.

After that question, I didn't teach or say anything more to the class. Instead, I turned to Marilyn Wilhelm and said, "You know, I think the wisest thing I could do right now is humble myself and sit down in that chair and listen to you. If the results are what you've done with this young man in three years, I would be far wiser to use my time listening to you."

Marilyn teaches her students nine languages; as well as the comparative arts, sciences, religions, and philosophies, and they understood them all. She may modify her vocabulary and language at times, but she sees these kids as geniuses, and they become what she envisions. Marilyn is one of the most energetic and vital people I've ever met. She loves what she does and does what she loves. She's a *teacher*, and she was called to this planet to teach.

I know that there's a part of you that has a calling, something you know deep down inside that you're here to do. Sometimes you don't want to face or acknowledge it, and sometimes you're frightened to death of it, but the reality is that you *know* what you're truly here for. Every circumstance, person, place, thing, idea, and event that occurs in your life is miraculously guiding, directing, and leading you to that special grand something that is powerfully inspiring for you.

We don't serve the world by shrinking, but by shining.

The Seven Areas of Life

You are here on this earth to master seven areas of life: spiritual, mental, vocational, financial, familial, social, and physical. They can either powerfully support your genius or impede it. Love in each of these areas can ignite your genius, but fear and guilt can cause them to smolder.

When you supply these areas with love, they become seven sources of power. The first is *spiritual power,* which is derived from having and honoring your spiritual mission. Would you agree that Gandhi, Christ, and Martin Luther King Jr., had a spiritual mission? People with such a mission have great power; they feel that God put them on this planet for a reason, and they're willing to fulfill it whether they live or die.

The second power is *mental genius,* which is a tremendous power. This is the power to know, to understand and solve problems. Albert Einstein, Isaac Newton, and Stephen Hawking are examples of people with extraordinary intelligence and power, and they've changed the world we live in.

The third power is *vocational,* involving career success. People such as George Lucas, Donald Trump, and Rupert Murdoch have the ability to affect the way the world thinks; and when they get an idea or a vision, they can implement it and make it real.

The fourth power is *financial.* I once consulted with a young woman (I'll call her Laura) whose new husband (I'll call him Steve) was the head of a major corporation. Steve's ex-wife (I'll call her Mary) was extremely angry that he had left her for Laura, but then Mary went on to marry another very wealthy man. Laura and her husband lived in the penthouse suite of a beautiful building with a fantastic view, so Mary said to her wealthy new husband, "I want you to build a tall building to block their view," and he did! Is that power? I'm not saying it's *smart* power, but money provides the freedom to do extraordinary things, and you're limited only by your vision.

The fifth power has to do with *family*—the power of a stable family and a deep, loving, mature relationship. Some call it a "dynasty," and it's a very powerful thing to develop and train an entire family to manage something great over many generations.

The sixth power is *social,* or the power of a social network. How many people do you know? How many know you? If you know a lot of people with influence, you can call them up and get things done; the larger your network, the greater your power.

The seventh power is that of *beauty and vitality.* Beautiful people definitely have a power. I got on an elevator once in Houston, and when the doors opened at the next floor, in came Miss Bolivia, Miss Brazil, and Miss Colombia, who later won the Miss Universe contest. I looked up at them, because they were taller than I was, and there was no question in my mind that they had real power.

The Seven Fears

Fear is the assumption that you're about to experience more pain than pleasure, more negative than positive, more loss than gain. Fear is an illusion that can fragment your full potential. There are seven fears, one for each of the seven areas of life.

The first fear is *spiritual*—being afraid of breaking morals and ethics. Morals are the rules that we with our internal society impose on ourselves, and ethics are the imposed rules between others and ourselves. Many people let these fears stop them from doing what they love because others may not approve of their actions. Some people are afraid to stand up for something because their religious community might reject them or God might strike them down.

The second fear is *mental*—worrying about not knowing enough. This fear can keep you from doing what you really love: "I'm not smart enough. I don't have the education for it." That's another illusion, because you have the capacity to do whatever you dream of doing at the level you're on now, and as you know more, you'll grow more. By loving yourself even when you don't know, you liberate yourself to learn.

The third fear is *vocational*—the fear of failure. Have you ever set goals and didn't fulfill them? Everyone has. You're a success and a failure continually throughout your life, and you need both. You must be able to love failure as much as success, since you fail and succeed equally and constantly. Baseball legend Babe Ruth held records for the most home runs *and* the most strikeouts, and that is the magnificence of this phenomenon. If you have a fantasy of only succeeding, you'll beat yourself up for being a failure, and then you'll ignore your balanced genius.

The fourth fear is *financial*. Here you fear that if you went out and did what you truly loved, you wouldn't make enough money at it. If you love something and are committed to doing whatever it takes to manifest it, value money highly, follow the proven laws of prosperity, and save, you can certainly build wealth.

The fifth fear is that *of losing your loved ones*. Many people feel that if they do what they love, they will *lose* someone they love. I think what stabilizes my marriage is that we don't so much *need* each other as we just *love* each other. There's a big difference. We both have independent lives, and if either of us were to leave, the other would still function. There's more a sharing than a "got to have them" form of desperation. Remember, if you probe deeply, nothing can be lost, only transformed.

The sixth fear is that of *social rejection*. This is a big fear. Some people aren't doing what they love because they're afraid that people will reject them. Since acceptance and rejection maintain balance, you can't receive one without the other. When you're able to love both equally, you're free. Praise and reprimand are conserved throughout your life, and the more extraordinary you become, the more you will receive of both. If you can't take the blame, don't expect the praise. I made up a principle called the Law of Lesser Pissers. It states that if you're given the choice between pissing someone else off or pissing yourself off, choose *them*. People come and go, but you're with you for the whole trip . . . and it's your life. Never sacrifice the eternal for the transient. Embrace both sides of life equally.

The seventh and last fear is that of *ill health, death, or disease.* Some people don't live their dreams because they're afraid they'll die if they do, or they won't have the energy. But the greatest cause of illness, disease, and death is *not* living your dreams. That will kill you quicker than anything else. Inspiration and gratitude heal and empower, and if you're not doing what you love, you'll feel ungrateful and desperate.

The difference between somebody who does what they love and someone who doesn't is that the former identifies their fears and has a strategy to break through them. When I was a little kid, I used to be terrified to walk into my room when it was dark. I was sure that there was a bogeyman in my closet, so I'd get my mom to turn the light on for me, and I'd walk in once I could see. That was when my dad gave me my first affirmation. He taught me to say, "I walk through the darkened doorway where fear lurks, and I actively turn on the light."

That's a pretty amazing thing for a father to give his five-year-old son, but I would repeat it over and over as I approached my room, then I'd jump in and . . . turnonthelight! With that little affirmation, he trained me to face the dark and turn on the light, and I still use it today . . . of course, not just to go into my room.

You can break through or break down in all seven areas of life. If you break down, you're listening to your fearful self; but if you break through, you've listened to your immortal self. Don't think you'll ever be without fears in your life; fear means you're growing and challenging yourself beyond your comfort zones. I have fears almost *every day*, but I know that fear is a lie, a lopsided perception clouding the hidden order; so I identify it, bring it to balance, then walk through it. It is then that I turn on my light.

"Forget about likes and dislikes, they are of no consequence. Just do what must be done. This may not be happiness, but it is greatness."
— George Bernard Shaw

I once had a biophysics teacher who, more than anything else in the world, wanted to know the origin of life. I saw him again just a few years ago. We had dinner at a Chinese restaurant, and I told him about my work, my research findings, and my beliefs concerning life coming from life. As I shared my thoughts, he suddenly got tears in his eyes and became choked up and speechless. I asked him what he was feeling or thinking.

He said, "You just reminded me of where I started 36 years ago with my work. I had an inspiration and wanted to dedicate my life to researching the origin of life, and I went from university to university because they wanted me to do so many other things that I wasn't interested in. I spend 80 percent of my energy writing research grant proposals, 10 percent teaching students, and only 10 percent on research."

He did what everybody else wanted him to do instead of what his heart was calling him to. He had an absolutely brilliant, specifically questioning mind, but because he didn't understand all seven areas of life and didn't want to value or master business or finances, he wasn't living his dream.

We can live lives of quiet desperation or . . . inspiration. This brilliant man had a shift at that moment because I told him that he had the power to open his heart and do what he loved if he would learn how to master the things he avoided. He might have to learn finances and business and become an entrepreneur, but the energy he invested would allow him to create his own research system and inspire others to join him in it. That woke him up, and he could see his dream again.

I ask people around the world what's stopping them from doing what they'd love to do in their lives, and they almost all say the same things: "I'd like to, but I don't have a degree. I'll do it when I finally get a relationship. I can't afford it. My husband or wife won't let me. I can't because nobody knows me and I don't have the contacts. If I did that, my church would disown me. I just don't have the energy."

There are excuses for every area of life. If you equilibrate your perceptions in each of those areas, you gain power; and if you dise-quilibrate them, you lower your potential. The Breakthrough Experience is about learning to go beyond limiting beliefs and emotions and going on to birth genius.

The Equilibrating Game

Have you ever noticed how the very instant you finally get your relationship together, something new falls apart? Or you get your career really happening and suddenly you have a health problem or a family crisis? Did you know that it's *designed* that way? Life takes you to ever-greater levels of understanding, and the fastest growth occurs right at the border of chaos and order.

Don't think, *Man, I really had things together there, but I lost it.* Realize that you've grown into the next level of chaos and are being given greater challenges because you have greater capacity. If you're sitting still in a life of ease, you're actually dis-easing, decaying, and breaking down. You want to constantly be on the edge of life. So don't sit back saying, "God, I wish life would get easier." Say, "I wish life would become more challenging, and I intend to *master* the skill of taking on even more of a challenge."

Make the embracing of new challenges your goal. That's the

secret of evolution—turning chaos and emotion into order and love so that you can take on even more and turn *that* into love. And there's no end to the chaos, the love, and the wisdom. You're never done. Some people think that they'll be finished when they're "enlightened," wealthy, or famous, but when they get there, *then* what?

Tapping in to your wisdom and genius means seeing both sides now—the chaos and the love—and not waiting for time to reveal the truth. You can have the wisdom of the ages without the aging process by balancing your mind *now*.

Imagine if you clearly defined exactly how you would express love in your life? What if you made a commitment to keep refining this goal and put it on a computer so it was more effectively and efficiently planned and fulfilled? What if you made visual pictures and audiotapes or CDs of it, put it on paper, and stuck it up all over your house, car, and business so that wherever you went you'd see it, think about it, and read it? What if you filled your day by associating with people who were absolutely inspiring; if you read biographies of the greats in the field you would love to master; watched their videos or listened to their tapes, CDs, or DVDs; and went to their exhibitions or live performances? Can you even imagine how that could rub off? You have divinity inside you, and you want to associate with those who feel divinely called to do what they do.

I had a dream that I would one day stand up and speak before some of the greatest teachers on Earth. I said, "I would love to be a teacher of teachers, a maestro of maestros," and I'm watching that gradually happen in my life. When I first stated it at a mastermind group, some of the partners said, "Oh, John, you're dreaming again," and I said, "You're absolutely right. I am." They couldn't see my vision quite as clearly as I could.

Many who can't see your dream will immediately try to ridicule you, or ask you to clarify how you'll fulfill it. It's part of the equilibrating game. Anybody who ridicules you also honors you by acknowledging that you have exceeded their capacity to understand what you're about. When people support you, they obviously think you can't do it on your own; but when they criticize you, it's an honor. If you could see all criticism as honor, would that be a motivation for you?

If you're infatuated with your dream, you'll also attract resentful, disowned parts to balance the infatuation. The difference is that if while they ridicule you, you embrace the challenge with clear vision and no emotional reaction, it's a sign that you're present with your dream. If while they ridicule you, you feel hurt or become emotionally defensive, then you're infatuated with your overexaggerated dream and require humbleness to moderate it and more effectively fulfill it. In either case, you grow.

Every moment we spend not focused on our dreams becomes a moment we spend focused on our doubts and obstacles. Every moment we spend not focused on the flowers, we're focused on the weeds. Geniuses focus on the ever-finer details of the flowers that emanate from their hearts, and they create a bouquet from their experiences. The average person who hasn't awakened their genius, who isn't even *aware* of it, is generally being distracted by weeds, doubts, and fears.

I have insecurities just like everybody else. Sometimes I feel like I'm a nobody, and that's part of the game, helping me equilibrate the part of me that thinks I'm a somebody. When I feel that way, I link my perceptions back to my purpose and see how those doubts are the driving force that keep me on the journey. They actually balance out the times when I think I can do *anything*, and keep me centered. It's okay to have those moments; they're not going to keep you from your dreams—they're gifts.

The weeds are inversely proportionate to how clear your flowers are. Obstacles are simply what you see when you take your mind off your focus. With every step you take toward the details of your dream, you become more creative, inspired, and ingenious. Everybody has a dream, but a genius is willing to define and redefine that dream and keep acting on high-priority actions to fulfill it.

Donald Trump was once asked in an interview, "You live a fantasy life, don't you?" and he replied, "No, I don't. A fantasy is something that you imagine but never live. I live my life of dreams. I live them, because I don't stop my planning and acting until I get them."

Fantasies are lopsided illusions to which we compare our reality; they eventually depress us. Dreams are realistic objectives that we refine our lives toward and can live.

Make a commitment that before you go to bed tonight, you'll take another action step toward your dream, because the clearer the vision, the greater the creative genius. Your vitality is directly proportionate to the vividness of your vision and the clarity of your calling, which are directly proportionate to how well you see and acknowledge the divine order. When you see perfect balance, the inner voice becomes loud and the inner vision becomes clear, and an incredible amount of energy is available to you. That's what gives you the courage, strength, and certainty to overcome your obstacles and keep rising, no matter what.

Exercise

Begin collecting and reading the biographies of the great geniuses of the world who inspire you: philosophers, actors, scientists, musicians, politicians, singers, writers, artists, composers—whatever the field. Read about the lives of those who have left an immortal legacy to humankind.

By immersing yourself in the lives of these geniuses, you'll carry some of that inspiration away with you. You'll find that not one of them was without the ups and downs, the supports and challenges, that fill your own life, and you'll be able to identify the common threads that made them extraordinary. It's impossible to put your hand into a pot of glue without some of that glue sticking. So, too, is it impossible to put your mind into the great works of genius without some of their genius sticking with you.

Words of Wisdom and Power

- *I talk to myself with the respect due a great genius.*
- *I look for the genius in everyone I meet.*
- *I link everything I do to my mission, and I am inspired by my life.*
- *I walk through the darkened doorway where fear lurks, and I turn on the light.*
- *I listen to my heart, which awakens my genius.*
- *My genius elevates me beyond my daily illusions.*

Chapter Nine

The Quantum Collapse Process

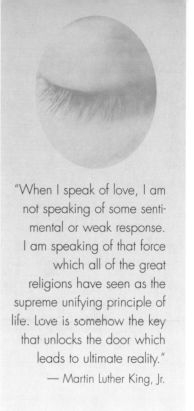

"When I speak of love, I am not speaking of some sentimental or weak response. I am speaking of that force which all of the great religions have seen as the supreme unifying principle of life. Love is somehow the key that unlocks the door which leads to ultimate reality."

— Martin Luther King, Jr.

The Quantum Collapse Process[1] is the most powerful tool I've found for dissolving illusions, centering the mind, opening the heart, and awakening inner vision and genius. Everything I've said so far has been leading to it, and this chapter is where it all comes together. If you follow it to completion, I guarantee that you'll have an experience that's impossible to deny or forget. You'll know that you've been blessed with a purpose, and everything in your life has been serving it. No matter what you've done or haven't done, your life is divine perfection. If you can truly comprehend that, you'll sit in awe in front of the Intelligence that governs us all. In that state, there's an unbounded potential energy, unfathomable to the normal mind, but available to those whose spirit is in a state of grace.

I'm about to teach you one of the most powerful processes you may ever find in your life, and if some part of you is thinking, *Well,*

---

[1]The Quantum Collapse Process™ is trademarked and copyrighted. Therefore it may be used for personal, not commercial, purposes. Without completing The Breakthrough Experience Annual Certification Training Program requirements, it is strictly forbidden to use this methodology for commercial purposes. For Information concerning The Quantum Collapse Process, The Breakthrough Experience, The Worldwide Certified Teachers or Training Certification simply call 1-888-DEMARTINI, or 713-850-1234, or fax 713-850-9239, or log on to: **www.drdemartini.com.**

there's not really anybody that pushes my buttons; I'm in control of my life, wake up! That's nonsense. You're here on this planet to grow, and anytime your ego thinks that you don't have anything pushing your buttons, you're living in a fantasy; otherwise you're not challenging yourself and allowing yourself to go to the edge. So find out who *is* pushing those buttons. It doesn't have to be somebody who enrages you; they can just make you feel distracted and not present. But doing Collapses on the people who have the biggest hook in you are the ones you'll get the most benefit from.

The purpose of this exercise is to balance out the lopsided perceptions that have been running your life, health, wealth, relationships, and self-worth, and free up your potential and inspired inner voice. I promise that if you go all the way to completion, that voice will speak to you. It's a science, and it works if you work it. The way I use it, the word *Collapse* does not mean to fall apart or lose strength. We're actually Collapsing your false beliefs and illusions about life. When your false nature Collapses, your true nature is revealed, and it's magnificent. Is that worthy of effort?

So, set aside three to five hours where you won't be interrupted, and go! Let nothing stop you. You'll be grateful!

Step 1

The first step in The Quantum Collapse Process is deciding whom you would love to do a Collapse on. Because of the compound association process mentioned in Chapter 4—the earlier someone appeared in your life, the closer they were to you, and the greater their effect on you—the more profound the domino effect will be after Collapsing them. If you have strong emotional charges and early associations with someone, they will affect everything downstream from that moment in time. For that reason, it's usually most powerful to begin with a parent.

But if you have a marriage or business partner who is high on your level of stress at this time, they're also a good start.

Consider these questions when making your choice:

- Who is running your life or burdening you the most?
- Who pushes your buttons the most?
- Who would you least like to be around?
- Who do you despise or resent or can't stand the most?
- Who are you "incomplete" with?
- Who "hurt" you?
- Who left, abandoned, or dumped you?
- Who are you having difficulty loving and would love to love more?
- Who do you perceive as being in your way?

For your first Collapse, it's best to choose someone outside of yourself, but ultimately it's going to be *you* reflected off somebody else anyway. There are things you deny that your personas won't let you see, but if you deal with their reflection in others, you'll soon see them in yourself more easily. Every Collapse is really a self-collapse at heart, because whatever you see out there is you. We don't love other people for their sake; we love them for our own.

The Quantum Collapse Process forms appear at the end of these instructions (I suggest you copy each form several times so you'll have extras), along with a condensed sample form to help you follow along. When you decide whom you want to Collapse, turn to the forms and write the person's name and today's date in the space provided at the top of the page.

Also write at the top of the page: "Every Person Has Every Trait" as a reminder. There are more than 4,000 human traits, and everybody has them in their own unique form, so don't imagine that you can't think of any when you're soon asked to write them; all you need to do is look.

Step 2

Okay, here we go! There are five columns on each page (starting on page 173), and you're going to be filling in at least four pages. (Note: You'll need to make copies of the pages in this book before beginnning.) You'll be doing at least two positive pages (Form A) and two negative pages (Form B) of what I'm about to show you. If you think you can't do it, quit thinking that; for the truth is you can. Anyone can do this process once they put their mind to it.

Go to Column 1 and write down the most *positive* and admirable trait about the person you can imagine, keeping it from one to four words long. For example, "Gave me gifts" or "Considerate." Continue listing the person's positive traits, writing only *one* trait in each of the rectangular boxes provided. Consider these questions as you look for positive traits:

- What human trait do you most like, admire, or consider positive or attractive about this person?
- What is it about this person that makes them likable?
- What has this person done or not done that feels so good?
- What is it about this person that makes you seek and admire them?
- Why is it that you feel so good when you think of them?
- Why can't you be away from them?
- Why do you want to deal with them or want to see them again?
- Why are you so attracted to them?
- Why do you desire them so much?
- What have they done or not done that you think you haven't or have?

Think in terms of chronology: What have they done or not done (past), are they doing or not doing (present), will they do or not do (future imagined), that was, is, or will be, pleasureful? Also think in terms of the seven categories or areas of life: spiritual, mental, vocational, financial, familial, social, and physical. Every human trait can be summarized and written into one, two, three, or four concise words.

Then go to Column 6 and write down the most *negative* and despised trait about your person you can imagine, in one to four words. For example, "Wasn't there for me" or "Stingy." Continue listing the person's negative traits, writing only one trait in each rectangular box. Make sure that the number of disliked traits you write in this column equals the number of liked traits you wrote in Column 1. Consider these questions when looking for the negative traits:

- What is it about this person that makes them unlikable?
- What has this person done or not done that feels so bad?
- What character trait do they demonstrate that pisses you off?
- What is it about this person that makes you avoid and despise them?
- Why is it that you hurt when you think of them?
- Why can't you be near them?
- Why don't you want to deal with them or want to see them again?
- Why do you despise them so much?
- What have they done or not done that you think you haven't or have?
- Why is it that you can't stand them?

Again, think in terms of chronology and the seven categories or areas of life. It's important to be specific about what you most admire or despise. Don't just say "Alcoholic," break it down, because it's probably not alcohol that you object to, it's probably all the components of alcoholism. Get specific. Was it yelling, physical roughness, no money, uncertainty, bad breath, mood swings, broken promises, shame, social stigma—what? The more specific you are, the easier it will be to dissolve. Get to the real meat, the intense stuff that pushes your buttons, and don't hold anything back. Remain focused. The bigger the charge and the more specific you can be, the better.

Fill in at least two pages of Columns 1 and 6, the positive and negative qualities or character traits of your person. If you have more than two pages, keep going. If you find yourself on a roll with one side, stay with it, but when it dries up, go to the other side and keep writing. Do whatever helps you move the fastest. Don't just sit there stagnating and staring. Time multiplied by intensity yields results, so the more focused you are, the more profound the effects. When you've filled at least two pages with positive and negative qualities, go on to the next step.

Step 3

Now go to Column 2 and write down the initials of all the people who have seen you as having the same positive and admired trait that you've written in Column 1. If you wrote "Considerate" there, put down the initials of all the people in your life that you know have perceived you as considerate at some point in time—past or present. Keep writing until you can see that you have the trait in Column 1 to the same degree as the person in question, although it may be in similar or different forms.

All of your traits are conserved through time and space, so you never gain or lose a trait; you only change the form of its expression.

Continue until you can honestly see that you're just as considerate as the person you're Collapsing. This is called *owning your positive disowned parts*. You may need as many as three rows of initials here, so write small. Don't just say "everybody," that's an illusion. Be specific. This is a way of integrating your brain and personas. If you think you don't have this trait, that's your illusion, so just keep thinking and writing until you can see that you do. I've been blessed to be able to assist more than 10,000 people through this process, and everyone finds every trait.

Now go to Column 7, writing down the initials of at least five people who have seen you as having the same negative and despised trait that you wrote down in Column 6. Find out who perceives you as having that negative trait, and list their initials until you can truly see that you have it to the same degree. On the average, it will be 5 to 8 people, but sometimes it will be up to 30 before this becomes confirmed with certainty. This step anchors into your mind the reality that you have these traits. It's essential to be honest with yourself. This is called *owning your negative disowned parts.*

If it's really obvious that you have a trait, you can put your own initials down, but don't stop there. Find out who else sees you that way. Don't live in the fantasy that nobody else knows or sees this trait in you, for that would be a form of self-denial of the trait. Thinking of where you do it can help you find out where somebody might see it in you.

If you have difficulty thinking of who sees you with some positive quality, that means that you're self-wrongeous and minimizing and beating yourself up in relation to it and them. If you have trouble seeing where you have the same negative quality, it means that you're self-righteous and exaggerating yourself and building yourself up in relation to it and them. Both the beating up and the building up create walls between you and your person, and between you and the truth. You've got the trait, it's just in a different form that keeps you from recognizing yourself in others.

Don't move on from any line in Columns 2 or 7 until you're absolutely clear that you have the same quality, to the *same degree*, as the person you're Collapsing. If you still think that they do it more than you, keep looking, otherwise you stay in self-righteousness or self-wrongeousness and hold yourself back. I promise you that it's not a matter of *if,* only a matter of *where* you have every quality.

There's no such thing as somebody being too hard; there's just somebody who reminds you of what you don't want to own inside yourself. Sometimes it seems too much to face about yourself, but this is a great opportunity to do exactly that. There are more than 4,000 human traits, and you've got them all in your own unique form and makeup. When you see that you have every quality you've listed in Columns 1 and 6, to exactly the same degree, go on to the next step.

Step 4

You've been working down vertically in these columns, but now I want you to go right across the page horizontally. If this is someone you resent, you're going to use Form B and do Columns 8, 9, and 10 next. If you're infatuated with them, you'll use Form A and do Columns 3, 4, and 5. If you're uncertain, you may want to do all six columns. This part may seem a little tricky at first, so you might want to follow along on the sample form.

If resentment and negativity are your dominant feelings when you think of this person, go to Column 8 and begin writing down how it benefits you that this person has that negative trait. Remember that whenever somebody is putting you down, somebody else is lifting you up; when someone withdraws from you, somebody else attaches to you; when somebody criticizes you, somebody else is praising you; when someone is being stingy to you, someone else is being generous. Keep the opposites in mind.

As you look at the first trait you wrote in Column 6, think of all the ways that this negative trait served you, and keep writing until you dissolve any hatred or resentment toward the trait. In our example, the negative trait in Column 6 is stinginess. How has this trait been a benefit? Well, the person in our example decided that it made them independent, considerate, creative, and realistic. It taught them to save and develop a financial strategy. Notice that these terms are all abbreviated on the sample form. Write just the first few letters, then move on to the next answer. Keeping your momentum up is an important part of this process. Don't stop until you can say, "Thank God they have this trait," and you have no more desire to avoid or change it.

Now go to Column 9 and ask yourself how *your* having that quality has served others. Some of the benefits will be the same as the ones you received when it was done to you, but don't stop writing here until all your guilt about doing it is dissolved through understanding, and you realize that you also served others by being that way. Once again, abbreviate your answers so you can keep writing quickly. For example, the person in our example saw that their being stingy offered the same benefits to others.

Then go to Column 10 and ask yourself about their *opposite* quality. Write the initials of everyone who observes or recognizes this opposite trait in them. If the negative quality was stinginess, then who has seen this person being generous? Keep writing until you can truly sense that the person in question has a perfect balance of trait and anti-trait. This can be a surprising and liberating column, showing how the traits are not only balanced but also accurate.

Then go to the second negative trait in Column 6 and repeat the same process in Columns 8, 9, and 10. Don't move on from any column until it's balanced, until you stop judging it as bad and experience gratitude for it. Repeat the process for the remaining negative traits until all the columns are filled and there's nothing left to judge your person for. You will experience little *Ahas!* of insight and tears of gratitude as you progress through your Collapse on the person you're attempting to love.

If you're infatuated with someone, just substitute Columns 3, 4, and 5, and follow the same procedure you used for the negative traits. For example, if the positive trait in Column 1 was "Considerate," you'd list the resulting drawbacks to you in Column 3. How is the trait in them a drawback or disservice to you? Did it make you feel guilty or like you had to give up some of your time for them? Did it make you feel obligated, dependent, or pressured? Was their attention a distraction to you? Keep writing until you dissolve any admiration or infatuation toward this trait. Don't stop until you see that the benefits and drawbacks are perfectly balanced and this trait no longer runs you.

Go on to Column 4 and find the drawbacks or disservice to others as a result of this trait in you.

Then do Column 5 to see where they displayed the opposite trait. Write the initials of everyone who observes or recognizes this opposite trait in them.

When you're done, go back to the remaining traits in Column 1 and repeat the process until all the traits in Column 1 are Collapsed into the balanced truth.

Additional Questions

Here are eight additional questions you may want to ask yourself while filling out The Quantum Collapse Process forms. They will assist you in completing Columns 1 to 10.

1. If this person did not have the human trait you dislike, what would be the drawback?

2. If this person did have the human trait you like, what would be the drawback?

3. If this person did not have the human trait you like, what would be the benefit?

4. If this person did have the human trait you dislike, what would be the benefit?

5. Who was acting out the opposite human trait of the one you dislike at the same moment?

6. Who was acting out the opposite human trait of the one you like at the same moment?

7. What human trait do you feel you miss, and what new form has this trait taken?

8. What human trait do you feel you have lost, and who now has taken on that trait?

You may be wondering, *How will I know when I'm finished?* Ask yourself, "What is still in the way of me loving this person?" and if you come up with even a tiny little fragment, take it through the questions in Columns 1 to 10 until you know beyond a shadow of a doubt that you appreciate and love the person. This sets you and them free.

At that moment, you'll feel the presence of the person you're conducting The Quantum Collapse Process on. You may have a visual image of them, hear their voice, sense them in some object in the room, or just feel them in your heart. That's the time to communicate your love and gratitude, to thank them for their gifts to you and the role they played in making you who you are. Pour it all out to them, and I promise that they'll get it in nonlocal communication. Then sit down and write them a thank-you letter, telling them how much you appreciate them and what a difference or contribution they made in your life. You may find yourself receiving even more insights when you do this. Writing is a powerful act that takes the intangible and makes it tangible.

You can make almost anybody on this planet get in contact with you by thoroughly completing The Quantum Collapse Process. The more you become present about them, and the more love and gratitude you feel, the more they will tune in to you and think of you, contact you, or transform in some way. And *you* will definitely be transformed by the experience. This process is quite enlightening and beautiful, just like the true you.

Sample Quantum Collapse Process™ Form — Side A

Column 1 Trait I most like about them	Column 2 The initials of who see this trait in me	Column 3 How this trait in them is a drawback to me	Column 4 How this trait in me is a drawback to others	Column 5 Initials of who see the opposite trait in them
Considerate	S, B, M, F, E, ST, CH, BL, Cl, U, A	Guilt, Time, Oblig., Dep., Press., Dist.	Guilt, Time, Oblig., Dep., Press., Dist.	CH, F, M, H, K, L, EM, CL, DR

Sample Quantum Collapse Process™ Form — Side B

Column 6 Trait I most dislike about them	Column 7 The initials of who see this trait in me	Column 8 How this trait in them is a benefit to me	Column 9 How this trait in me is a benefit to others	Column 10 Initials of who see the opposite trait in them
Stingy	T, G M, S, R, ST, C, BL, F, JD, B	Indep., Cons., Creat., Real., Save, Strat.	Indep., Cons., Creat., Real., Save, Strat.	P, T, D, L, R, G, M, ED, CH, DR

Note to reader: Please make multiple copies of the following forms before you fill them out so you will have plenty for future use.

The Quantum Collapse Process™ Form, Side A

Person: _____ Date: ___/___/___

Column 1 Trait I most like about them	Column 2 Initials of who see this trait in me	Column 3 How this trait in them is a draw- back to me	Column 4 How this trait in me is a drawback to others	Column 5 Initials of who see the opposite trait in them

Seven Areas of Life: Spiritual Mental Vocational Financial Familial Social Physical **Think:** Past Present Future
When positives outweigh the negatives, you become emotionally attracted and infatuated (addicted).
When positives don't equal negatives, you lie. Lies are imbalances.
When positives equal negatives, you become grateful and unconditionally loving. The truth is balance!

The Quantum Collapse Process™ Form, Side B

Person: _____ Date: ___/___/___

Column 6 Trait I most dis-like about them	Column 7 Initials of who see this trait in me	Column 8 How this trait in them is a benefit to me	Column 9 How this trait in me is a benefit to others	Column 10 Initials of who see the opposite trait in them

Seven Areas of Life: Spiritual Mental Vocational Financial Familial Social Physical **Think:** Past Present Future
When negatives outweigh the positives, you become emotionally repelled and resentful (subdicted).
When negatives don't equal positives, you lie. Lies are imbalances.
When negatives equal positives, you become grateful and unconditionally loving. The truth is balance!

Thank-You Letter

Write a thank-you letter to the person you completed "The Quantum Collapse Process" on.

_____

_____

_____

_____

_____

_____

_____

_____

_____

_____

_____

_____

_____

_____

_____

_____

_____

_____

_____

_____

_____

_____

_____

_____

_____

_____

This is a letter I recently received from a lady in Australia about her experience of The Quantum Collapse Process. I think it speaks for itself.

Dear John,

I was a participant in your Breakthrough Experience in Sydney. I experienced a major shift in my psychology on that weekend and had quite a profound Collapse. Even though this Collapse felt truthful at the time, I still came away wondering if perhaps I had fudged it in some way. I decided I really needed to speak to the person I Collapsed and tell her, as I had done on Saturday night, how much I loved her and thank her for all she has done for me. The time came on Monday for me to go to her house. I was really scared, butterflies going crazy, and again I was wondering, "If I am this scared, have I truly completed my Collapse or have I got more work to do here?" I took a deep breath and drove to her house, as if drawn there by a magnet. I knew deep down she would be there. I went inside, and before I could really say anything to her, we just looked into each other's eyes and both started to cry. We stood there and embraced, and I told her how much I loved her and thanked her for being her. She said she had wanted to tell me the same thing for some time. It was one of the most profound, loving moments I have experienced in my life, and it happened exactly as you said it would, I just couldn't see her without love. The most amazing thing was that she was waiting for me to come. If I hadn't gone there, she was going to come to me.

I have for a long time been wondering why the search for positiveness and happiness has felt so elusive. That even in the midst of living what I feel is a pretty wonderful life, I have always had an underlying feeling that it was all temporary and that disaster was waiting just around the corner, especially after experiences of happy highs. Now I understand these feelings to a higher degree, and it's such a huge relief. Now I understand that trying to be positive in my outlook all the time and trying to be happy all the time is just a myth. It's an amazing revelation and an inspiration to do some hard work to find my true destiny and work toward creating it.

I want to thank you for such a revealing, confronting, inspiring, loving, and magnificent weekend. Without all of your incredible wisdom and hard work over the years to develop your amazing philosophy of human existence and your dedication to The Breakthrough Experience, I certainly wouldn't be where I am today. I thank you for opening my eyes to the truth and giving me the opportunity to live a more loving life.

Thank you.

It's Your Sister

I was presenting The Breakthrough Experience in my office about a decade ago. Attending was a gentleman named David who decided to Collapse his sister. They had basically disowned each other and had had no contact whatsoever for 11 years. As far as he was concerned, she was no longer in his family. He decided to do the Collapse on her because he was still so angry with her.

He began to work on the columns as I've just described, and he finished his Collapse on her at about 11 o'clock that night. To assist him, I had him choose a surrogate woman who reminded him of and represented his sister. He held her hand, embraced her, and communicated his love and appreciation for her. At precisely the moment he embraced her, the telephone in my office rang.

When David finished communicating with the surrogate lady, we went to the phone and listened to the message. The voice said, "Is David there? Please have him call me. This is his sister." As he got the full realization that it was his sister, we literally had to hold him up, he was crying so hard. And it was an entirely different voice than he had remembered. It was receptive, open, and loving. She just wanted to reach her brother.

He contacted her later and their relationship completely shifted, after 11 years, because of the completion, love, and integration inside him. He had identified enough detail about his sister during the Collapse to tune in to her frequency, and when you do that, it's just like calling somebody. You have access to anybody, even those some have labeled "dead."

The Quantum Collapse Process is not always easy to complete, but it's unbelievably powerful. Nothing worthwhile is ever easy. Your personas will do whatever they can to not have you complete it, because they don't want to lose their power over you and "die" by being merged or integrated back into your consciousness. You may find yourself being easily distracted or getting hungry, tired, or impatient. Your mind will get vague and dreamy or go completely blank, and you'll tell yourself it's too hard, it doesn't work, or you can't do it. You'll swear you don't possess the traits or qualities the person has, or that you've already forgiven or loved them for it. All those reactions and more will try to block you. In fact, the closer you get to the truth, the more your personas will react, so take these avoidance symptoms as a sign that you're completely on target!

I won't be there to help you, but if you simply stay with it until it's completed, the rewards will be vast compared to the effort. It's up to you to master yourself. It can take hours of concentrated effort, but so what? How many hours have you spent watching TV, reading, driving, or doing some trivial, less purposeful act? What else are you going to do with your life that's more important than opening your heart and truly loving, possibly for the first time? What's more important than having your inner voice of certainty and inspiration speak to you, and knowing beyond all question that no matter what you've done or haven't done, you're worthy of love? Do your best with the Collapse. Try to complete it all in one session, but if you can't, then come back to it at frequent intervals and keep going. It's worth more than you can imagine until it happens for you.

Signs of Wisdom and Illumination

If you're still not sure whether you experienced a complete Collapse, here are some of the phenomena and noumena that consistently follow The Quantum Collapse Process. Over and over again, I see the same signs in people whenever their hearts are wide open. The more open the heart, the more profound the experience.

1. *Tears of inspiration.* I've worked with people from 37 countries around the world, and it doesn't matter what culture they're from, tears of inspiration consistently appear when the mind reaches perfect equilibrium. This is not emotion, it's *love.* I want you to distinguish them: emotions are polarized; love is synthesized. Tears of inspiration demand respect. When someone is in gratitude and awe, is inspired, and has opened their heart, you can't *help* but honor and revere them.

2. *Growth in self-worth.* Every time you love another individual, you increase your self-worth. The real and true spiritual experience is having a moment of grace and communion with your soul, and feeling the presence of God directing your life. That's what it's about, and we all have access to it. It doesn't matter what race, creed, color, faith, or age you are—none of that is significant. Those are merely shells and personas overriding the true spiritual life, and this is a science of that life.

3. *Unconditional gratitude.* Looking at the person for whom you've filled out The Quantum Collapse Process, you can't perceive anything that you're not grateful for. There's nothing left to judge. You feel true gratitude for them just the way they are, without any conditions—not as they should be, might become, or sometimes were, but gratitude for them just as they are. You just feel as if you would love to say, "Thank you. I truly appreciate you."

4. *Unconditional love.* You now have a depth of love for this person that nobody could shake or argue away. Nothing outside can touch it. In this state, your mind can become so attuned to undifferentiated Divinity that you receive direct or indirect divine revelation. That's the highest state the human psyche can achieve, and it's where masterpieces are birthed. This is where new religions, great prose and poetry, and great music and art are created—all in this realm of reception and unconditional love.

5. *Fearlessness and guiltlessness.* If you still say, "I'm so sorry for what I did," or "I just wish they'd say they're sorry," you're still clinging to the lopsided, pain-inducing perceptions of fear or guilt. Pain is a private sensation of hurt based on perceptual associations that are either positive or negative. If they're lopsided to the negative/pain side, you'll experience pain; and if they're lopsided to the positive/pleasure side, you'll experience pleasure. It's a choice. When your perceptions are balanced, fearlessness and guiltlessness result.

6. *Speechlessness and outward silence.* You'll reach a point where there's nothing to say, where you just feel pulled to silently embrace the person you love. To speak is often to distort truth. The last words before the truth of silence are: "Thank you. I love you."

7. *Reduced inner brain noise.* Brain noise is the conscious and unconscious chatter that fills your mind. It's directly proportional to how many bipolar fragmented personas you have inside. The personas are talking, and the greater the number of lies, the more unclear your consciousness. After completing The Quantum Collapse Process, your brain becomes clear and the personas are neutralized, integrated, and quiet. The only voice left to speak is that of your enlightened soul.

8. *Balance, centeredness, and integration.* If your mind becomes perfectly balanced, you feel centered and more integrated. Your many bipolar personas become fewer in number and greater in consciousness. Your power rises, and so does your certainty and presence. Your body tone balances. Your physiology normalizes and you heal.

9. *Lightness and weightlessness.* You may feel like you've released a burden or taken a weight off. It's the difference between feeling on top of the world and having the world on your shoulders. Clients have actually lost weight from this process, because a big part of weight gain is emotional charge. Reduce the charge and reduce the weight.

10. *Nonlocal, all-sense presence of the loved one.* If the mind is perfectly centered and balanced, local space and time perceptions disappear, and you enter a world of nonlocality. That's where you have access to anybody, alive or "dead," at any time and in any place. This is mystical, the Christ or Buddha experience. You enter the realm of the unfathomable, esoteric world. The self-righteous and self-wrongeous personas live in the exoteric state of consciousness, but the soul lives in the esoteric world.

11. *Experience of light.* If you go all the way into a thorough and profound Collapse and become fully open-hearted, you'll have the unforgettable experience of light. A gentleman in California did a Collapse on himself and had such an illuminating experience that the people in the room shared in it. He and the man he chose to represent himself literally emanated an amazing exchange of light. I hope you reach this state at least once so you'll know the truth of your spiritual light.

12. *Certainty of truth.* You know with clarity and an unshakable certainty that you truly love the person you Collapsed. You recognize that there is one great truth, that the universe is filled with love, and all else is an illusion.

13. *Desire to embrace.* You feel irresistibly drawn to the person you Collapsed because your repulsive charges that keep people out are gone. The walls have come down, all fear is gone, and you feel an overwhelming calling to embrace the loved one.

14. *Uplifting of the head and eyes.* People around the world spontaneously raise their eyes upward, as if they were looking to something greater above and beyond. You tend to look up and say, "Thank you, universe," because you realize that you, with all your knowledge and experience of life, didn't understand how it was all beautifully ordered. You now sense the underlying intelligent order, and you gratefully humble yourself to this hidden Intelligence that is greater than yourself.

15. *Domino effect of fuller understanding of past events.* You look back over your life and begin to see how everything makes sense. You see the balance and make the connections, and you say, "My God! No wonder that occurred in my life, and no wonder that happened. No wonder my father was like that. Now I understand."

All of these things happen because this is a science of physiology and spirit, and you can't override it with your mind. You can choose to not complete The Quantum Collapse Process, but if you do choose to take your mind to a threshold of perfect balance, tears of inspiration and gratitude will come out, and degrees of everything else listed above will manifest in proportion to your gratitude. It doesn't matter who or where you are, it simply happens. It is a reproducible science that I call the "scientific ritual."

Your life in this world eventually undergoes a sort of natural Collapse Process. You can't escape it. Positive things inevitably reveal their negative side, and negative things reveal their positive side. The Breakthrough Experience and The Quantum Collapse Process were designed to reunite all your illusions, lies, and personas back into the one light of your true spirit, to let you hear the inner voice and accomplish what you were put on Earth to do. The only difference is the time frame. I'm offering you the wisdom of the ages without the aging process.

Last, I encourage you to attend The Breakthrough Experience seminar live either with me or one of my certified teachers and ask all of the questions that this book has raised in your mind. Confront me with any of your uncertainties about this method or its principles. I'm certain that I can help you find the blessings to your challenging experiences, and help you truly experience your own magnificence. You'll experience everything I've shared so far, and more. You owe it to yourself to not let this opportunity go by.

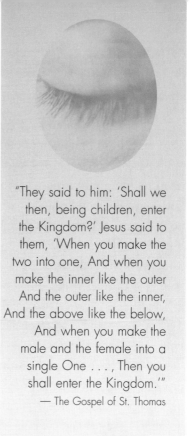

Chapter Ten

Conception: Believing Is Seeing

"They said to him: 'Shall we then, being children, enter the Kingdom?' Jesus said to them, 'When you make the two into one, And when you make the inner like the outer And the outer like the inner, And the above like the below, And when you make the male and the female into a single One . . . , Then you shall enter the Kingdom.'"

— The Gospel of St. Thomas

From the source of wisdom within your soul, through your enlightened heart and mind, come inspired visions, messages, and feelings. When you're inspired and ask your inner voice or soul to guide you, it provides infallible direction. Being in a state of gratitude will open your heart and help you know what you would love to be, do, and have in your life. After completing The Quantum Collapse Process, you're in this state of gratitude and love, the perfect state to listen to your heart and write or type out your most inspiring dreams and goals. I call this "The Love List," and in the pages that follow, I'm going to show you exactly how to create your own.

What if your life turned out the way you dreamed and planned it? If you knew you couldn't fail, if you listened to your heart and soul and wrote down exactly what you would love to be, do, and have in all seven areas of life, what would that be? You'd produce a Love List that provided clear, specific information about your direction, making it easier to manifest in your life.

Let me give you an analogy to show you what I mean. Imagine you're the head of a team of builders and I'm an architect who wants you to erect a building. If I said to you and your crew, "Go construct a tall building in downtown New York," could you do it? Of course not! You can't build it unless you know every single detail—the purpose, location, number of floors, materials, design, cost, timetable, everything. But what if I say, "Okay, I want you to build it on Wall Street. It's 100 stories high, 100 feet wide, and 100 feet deep. It's made out of steel with cement floors, and it's going to be faced magnificently with black marble, polished steel, and glass. There's going to be a spa on the 20th floor and another on the 50th floor." Are you getting a clearer picture?

"It will have perfect security to protect the tenants, with fingerprint and retinal scanners. There will be indoor gardens, a tennis court and helipad on the roof, and a 10,000-square-foot penthouse. It's going to have private cleaning, limousine, and travel services, and it will be erected at the rate of one floor per week. The foundation will be 60 feet deep, and we'll begin in two weeks." As I provide more details, do you start to see it? Can you see that any questions or obstacles that you might have are exactly the details I leave out?

In much the same way, your uncertainty in life is directly proportionate to the details that you haven't questioned and answered. If you want to achieve self-mastery, you must ask the questions and get the details to master your life or you won't build it. The question is, are you important enough to yourself to take the time to plan?

Fail to Plan, Plan to Fail

As Mies van der Rohe said, "God is in the details." An inspired vision isn't just some vague perception; it must be extremely clear and detailed. The vision I had on the plane years ago for The

Breakthrough Experience was very detailed, and sometime later I had a vision for a book that included the content, the color, the cover, the type style, the paper stock—every last detail. It was as if I could pick up that book in my mind and read it. That is the clear detail I'm talking about.

Your Love List must be specific enough so that anybody else could grab it and act. The higher the degree of specificity, the higher the probability that you'll live it.

I have a personal book filled with specific details of exactly how I would love my life to be. I find that the more I read and refine this book, the more my dreams manifest in accordance with those details. Imagine that you've been given the responsibility to build each of the seven areas of your life, you've been provided with a whole group of people to help you, and the more detail you have, the bigger the crew you will be provided. Without your detailed direction, they won't know what to do; uncertainty arises, and you have to lay them off because there's not enough work.

In this creation process, you have a balance between *making* things happen and *letting* things happen. It's wise to lay out a plan, but not to be so rigid with it that you can't allow refinement and adaptation. Many of my goals are highly specific and specifically articulated, but with some I leave the manner of their manifestation quite open. The purpose of the plan isn't necessarily to make it go only that way, but to allow your mind to see it clearly enough to erase all fear and doubt. Then you can attract what you envisioned, or even more efficient alternatives.

Some people set up a wildly ambitious plan and a totally unrealistic time frame with their self-righteous persona rather than with their true openhearted being. When the plan doesn't materialize, they feel depressed. If you set a goal with your self-righteous persona, you're going to get *burned out* attempting to accomplish it. If you set it with your self-wrongeous persona, you won't be motivated and you'll be *bored in*. Inspiring visions that are crystal clear can be manifested. You don't get elated or depressed about them; you just keep working away until they materialize.

Every heart contains a plan, but you may not have put yours on paper yet. Your detailed master plan or blueprint for life is your mortal self's attempt to fulfill your immortally gifted divine design. Some of my divine designs are clear; they come to me and I get tears in my eyes as I see the whole picture. There's no question, and so I just do it. Sometimes the plan takes years to fully materialize, but I know I am to do it, so I just keep working.

If you have to ask the question, "Is this what I would love?" it isn't. Instead, it's some exaggerated or minimized goal set by your self-righteous or self-wrongeous persona. It's one that will require refinement in the form of additions or deletions. If it's purely inspired, then there's nothing to change; it just shines through.

Flexibility

Along my journey, I have set a series of goals that I eventually complete and delete or simply adjust. Sometimes I set goals partially through the influence of my personas, and I must refine and adjust them. My intuition lets me know when that happens, and I train myself to listen to it. Your intuition will let you know when your plan requires refinement or editing, too. Look and listen for the quiet and certain knowing that comes with the tears in your eyes.

Some of the goals that you write on your Love List aren't necessarily meant to be completed. They're brought into your consciousness to get you to an experience that takes you to the next goal. You might set a goal and stay on track with it for three months, and then suddenly learn something that you wouldn't have learned except by following that path. You shift course, reassess your pathway, and say,

"It's not essential that I complete this goal. It was merely a stepping-stone to a greater realization. If I hadn't written it down earlier and worked toward it, I wouldn't have had this new and more efficient realization." It's still perfectly in line with your dreams, and part of the divine perfection.

Your list of visions and loves isn't set in stone. It's never done. If you see something you can tweak and refine tomorrow or next week, do it. I've been on boards of companies where some of the plans take two or three years to put together. We work on them, restructure and refine them, and keep playing with them until they're clear. Only then does efficient action begin. Your Love List should be an ongoing evolutionary structure of where you're going and what you're building in your life. As you become more aware, you add new layers. You don't want to be too rigid. Whatever the vision, it's wise to say, "Either this, or something even more efficient," to allow the universe to bring input to your dreams. This is the beginning of the master plan to create the masterpiece that's called your life.

Vision Is Life

The wise men of Greece used to teach their students philosophy and astronomy. The nearby statesmen with narrower viewpoints would ask why they wasted time teaching such abstract thinking to the youth.

The wise men would reply, "Students who study only practical matters don't develop a broad enough vision to extend beyond themselves. They must be stretched and made uncomfortable to get out beyond their normal realm of thinking." The theoretical and abstract are just as essential for a fulfilling life as the practical and concrete. They involve the immortal that drives and extends the mortal.

"The real voyage of discovery consists not in seeking new landscapes, but in having new eyes."
— Marcel Proust

When you write your Love List, I recommend that you include short-term goals that are specific, detailed, and that can be easily accomplished; long-term goals that are possibly a little less clear but will be revealed as you go along; and visions for your entire life.

I consulted with a doctor a few years ago whose dream was to open up a health clinic, have many doctors work with him, teach other doctors how to run a series of his clinics, create a school for teaching doctors how to run single or multiple clinics, then create a major school that was debt-free, self-sufficient, and able to carry on beyond his life. He accomplished every single one of his goals. Shortly afterward, though, he had a stroke. I sat down with him a few days after the stroke, which psychosomatically represented a state of futility, a loss of will to push on, and no more details left within his life vision. I worked with him for several hours attempting to draw out of him some further vision or next step for his life, but he stubbornly declared that he was done.

Prior to our meeting, he'd been going through a divorce where his wife received almost everything and tried to get ownership of his school. When we met, he was deathly angry. It was too much for him to be able to take in and love. He was so angry and mentally distracted that his board of directors voted him out of his presidency, leaving him surrounded by controversy and family concerns. At that point, he thought, *Well, why bother anymore?* His death wish became greater than his life wish. He saw no point in going any further and died a few weeks later.

Retirement can have that effect on some people who work their whole lives just to stop working. As the Book of Proverbs says, "Where there is no vision, the people perish." I think it's wiser to say,

"I plan to live my life fully until the moment I stop breathing, being productive and doing something that fulfills me and serves others."

Paul Bragg had me plan my life until I was at least 100 years old, but I'm beginning to think that won't be long enough. At age 47, I'm building momentum as I unfold my life's vision, and I'm beginning to plan goals that extend way into the future.

Whether you realize it or not, you have a yearning for immortality in every area of your life. You want offspring, subordinates, or students who live on beyond you; and somebody to carry on your name, energy, or experiences. You want to leave some effect on society so that they remember you, and wouldn't you like to end up with more money at the end of your life than life at the end of your money? Your spirit knows this and is doing whatever it can to wake you up to your dreams and your true worth, but you must listen to it.

The Slinky Principle

To write on your Love List exaggerated goals that you're unable to bring to practical reality is to let your self-righteous persona rule you. Burnout can occur this way. When you're not doing what you love or loving what you do, and you try to let your exaggerating persona set your goals, you probably won't live up to these goals. Consequently, you'll be left feeling overwhelmed. I use this analogy: Life is like a Slinky®, and you're on a journey walking along its coils. When you're self-righteous, the Slinky bobs up; and when you're self-wrongeous, it dips down. When it's bobbing up or dipping down, you have to hold on to the Slinky. You don't get to walk unless you're balanced, steady, and centered.

Details keep you centered, balanced, and moving forward. You reach divinity through infinite detail, because as you focus on the details, you become more present with your creations and steadier with your actions. You are a co-creator in a universal system. If your plan is detailed enough, you'll draw in the people who will help make it happen. The more vague and hesitant the plan, the more chaos and frustration you experience just trying to get to it. So, go for the details!

That's exactly what a friend of mine named Mark Victor Hansen has done. Almost 18 years ago, we were both at Bally's Hotel in Las Vegas to speak at a convention. One night, he told me, "John, I want to share one of my dreams with you, and I want to hear yours." He went on to say, "Someday I want to have a phenomenal, runaway, bestselling book filled with inspiring stories that open people's hearts, a book that sells millions and millions of copies, like nothing ever before on the face of the earth."

Mark had a detailed plan. He cut out pictures of book covers from the *New York Times* bestseller list and looked for what they had in common. When his book first came out, he arranged copies of it into a big pile and took a lot of photos and stuck them together in a collage until he had an image of a million books. Then he superimposed a picture of Oprah Winfrey into one with himself, his co-author Jack Canfield, and a huge stack of their books. He added a chicken with a bowl of soup at the bottom, and he sent copies to strategic people including his publicist and everybody he could think of who might assist him in the fulfillment of his dreams.

Chicken Soup for the Soul has now sold millions and millions of copies, in all its editions. There are even greeting cards and a TV show based on the book. And to think it started almost 18 years ago when Mark declared his dream and became clear about the details of how he would love it. Mark is a most inspiring visionary and an amazing man to meet.

I visited Mark's publicist's office a few years ago, and there was that big poster of Mark and Jack standing with Oprah Winfrey and a million books in the background. Do you know why? To remind him that every detail he didn't focus on could become his obstacle.

I wonder what would happen if we were to focus on the details in our own lives, just like Mark did.

Soul Seeds

The people who leave immortal effects are the ones who discover the universal principles and apply them, no matter what. At first, any new skill is a challenge to master. When you first learn to read or write, it's difficult. I was left-handed in first grade when left-handedness wasn't permitted. I also had my left foot and arm in a brace. I wrote backwards, and I was dyslexic. But today my hand is straight, and so is my foot. I love learning, I teach speed reading, and I'm an author who lectures around the world.

I don't think there's been a day in 29 years that I haven't written down some part of my dream. I have my book of dreams, affirmations, and visual images, and every single day I update on my computer exactly how I would love my life to be. I realize that every moment I do that, as I set out my master plan to match the divine design of life, I empower myself to create and fulfill my destiny. Nobody else is going to do it for me. As my old next-door neighbor Mrs. Grubbs once said, I would much rather be planting and smelling flowers than pulling weeds. So my Love List and dreams are up to me.

When I was 17, Paul Bragg helped me receive a revelation for my life. He made such an impact on me that I have never been the same. Ever since that moment, it's been my dream to have the same effect on others. Meeting someone who'd studied universal laws himself and seeing how much he wanted to share them meant everything to me. I thought, *God, I would love to do that. That would be fulfilling to me, to know that I'd made an impact on people's lives and helped them find their dream and fulfill it.*

Not even halfway through my life, I'm already on track with this aim, and I'm fulfilling my dreams. When I'm 93 years old, I'm going to have a group of 17-year-old students sitting in front of me, and I'll share with them the essence of what I've been able to learn. I've dedicated my life to preparing for this. I may be a crumpled-up little old guy, but no matter what, I'm going to share that inspiration. I know I'm going to pass the torch, and there will be a 17-year-old young man and woman sitting in that class to take it and stand on my shoulders, and they're going to do something magnificent. I know it because I see it, and in my mind, it has already happened.

You may have an Academy Award to receive, a gold medal to win, a book to write, something to create, a family to raise, a career to build, a fortune to amass . . . I don't know what your dream is, but *you* do, and by God, don't let anything on the face of this earth stop you. Don't let any person, place, thing, idea, or event stop you from having that dream, because that's what life is about. It's made out of your spiritual calling, brought into physical reality.

"I expect to pass through this world but once.
Any good therefore that I can do, or any kindness that
I can show to my fellow creature, let me do it now. Let me
not defer or neglect it, for I shall not pass this way again."
— Attributed to Stephen Grellet

Imagine if you dedicated your life to your dream and let nothing, and I mean *nothing* stop you. If you let no person on the planet, no challenge, obstacles, fears, or emotions stop you from being exactly what you dream about, how could it not come true? There's nothing more inspiring in my life than to speak to people who are willing and receptive, sharing from my heart the keys to a magnificent life. I only hope there's a part inside of you that resonates with these principles and sees your true and unbounded potential.

The most magnificent thing in life is to be able to get up every morning and do what you love and love what you do, to be well paid and inspired to do it, to make your vacation your vocation. I hope that somehow I've touched and seeded that part inside your heart so that you'll be able to live your dream as I live mine.

If I can convince you to write down your dreams every single day, to read and visualize and affirm them, to focus on and feel called to them, I guarantee that someday you'll say, "I remember the day I began, and it was all true. I'm living my dreams."

Fill your mind and days with those dreams, and they'll become your life.

Setting Your Own Course

A few years ago, a gentleman came to my program and said, "I've been a physician all my life because my father was a doctor, and it was the thing to do in our family. But he's passed away now and I don't have to prove anything to him. My real heart's dream has always been to be a professional golfer—can you help me with this?"

Just like with Miss Houston, I asked him, "What do you see?" and got him to describe his dream in detail. When he spoke about his golfing, he actually got tears in his eyes; he was truly inspired about it, it's what he loved. So together we laid out a blueprint for him to make his dream come true.

I said, "Make a list of the greatest golfers in the world, and plan to meet them all. Then make a sacred room in your house, and put every imaginable thing that inspires you about golf in that room. Find every video or picture of anybody who's ever made a hole in one, set a course record, won a championship, come back from defeat, or taken a title at an advanced age, and put them in this room. Visualize yourself being a golfer, and repeat affirmations that strengthen your certainty about it."

He went even further than I expected. He bought a virtual golf program that creates the experience of playing golf with unbelievable detail. He cut out pictures of his face and stuck them on the covers of all the top golf magazines so he could see himself holding big trophies. Knowing that the people you meet make a difference in your life, he compiled a list of the top golfers and made it a goal to meet them all. He practiced every day, visualizing himself making holes in one; and he filled his life with the visual pictures, affirmations, and technology that aligned with his dream. He took leave from his practice and moved to Florida, where he successfully traded in the stock market for a few hours a day and just golfed the rest of the time. He is now a professional golfer on the circuit, making a great living.

He decided that he was worth his dream. He took the time to work out exactly how he would love to live his life. Unlike many other people, he willingly did whatever it took, traveled whatever distance, and paid whatever price. Most people are too busy to take the time to plan, and they're distracted by low-priority actions instead of committing themselves to high-priority dreams.

With every step we take toward the details of our dream, we become more creative, inspired, and ingenious. A genius is one who is willing to define and refine their dream, and keep acting on high-priority actions to fulfill it. Someone with a mission that extends far greater than any concern of success or failure is unstoppable. That man wasn't worried about whether he gained or lost; he was only interested in mastering and fulfilling what he felt was his destiny. He felt called to be a golfer, and in a remarkably short time, he accomplished his dream.

Your Love List

Most people have never taken the time to ask themselves, "What would I truly love to do with my life?" Not what they *can*, *should*, or *must* do, but what they would *love* to do. The quality of your life is determined by the quality of the questions you ask. If you keep asking yourself that question and don't stop until you get the answers—and keep refining those answers—you will awaken to and create a magnificent life.

It's time to write your Love List. This is going to be your initial draft. I recommend that you put it on a computer and consistently upgrade and refine it as you get more details, which will come to you if you take it seriously and understand its impact. Make each statement clear and specific. Nebulous, general statements such as "I want to be happy, I want to be successful, I want to be spiritual" create a nebulous, general life. If you want to be spiritual, you must define it: Do you mean praying, meditating, glowing, what? Does success mean a certain amount of money, travel, prestige, having something, meeting somebody?

Without this level of detail, your plan will be too nebulous to act on, and if you don't act, you're just writing empty words. The greater your detail, the more tremendous your creative power.

Here's an example of some detailed and specific statements:

Be: A wealthy multimillionaire and charitable philanthropist by age 40.

Do: A monthly accelerated savings plan where I invest $2,000, then $3,000, then $4,000, and so on, with the Merrill Lynch financial brokerage corporation using the strategy of dollar-cost averaging combined with value averaging, continually building cushions of investment classes while diversified through sectors, using a balance of actively managed mutual funds and passively managed index funds.

Have: Patience and the rewards of financial freedom, travel, and social and charitable opportunity.

Are you ready to write your Love List? For each of the seven areas of life, consider what you want to *be, do,* and *have.* Write specific, detailed statements:

SPIRITUAL

Be:_____

_____

_____

_____

_____

_____

Do:_____

_____

_____

_____

_____

_____

Have:_____

_____

_____

_____

_____

_____

MENTAL

Be:_____

_____

_____

_____

_____

_____

Do:_____

_____

_____

_____

_____

_____

Have:_____

_____

_____

_____

_____

_____

VOCATIONAL

Be:_____

_____

_____

_____

_____

_____

Do:_____

_____

_____

_____

_____

Have:_____

_____

_____

_____

_____

FINANCIAL

Be:_____

_____

_____

_____

_____

_____

Do:_____

_____

_____

_____

_____

_____

Have:_____

_____

_____

_____

_____

_____

FAMILIAL

Be:_____

_____

_____

_____

_____

_____

Do:_____

_____

_____

_____

_____

_____

Have:_____

_____

_____

_____

_____

_____

SOCIAL

Be:_____

_____

_____

_____

_____

_____

Do:_____

_____

_____

_____

_____

_____

Have:_____

_____

_____

_____

_____

_____

PHYSICAL

Be:_____

_____

_____

_____

_____

_____

Do:_____

_____

_____

_____

_____

_____

Have:_____

_____

_____

_____

_____

_____

Once you've written your *be, do,* and *have* statements, you may want to refine the components into an overall plan. Here's a sample:

Dear God, I ask that I forever remain an inquisitive explorer— one determined to solve some of humanity's natural riddles, one willing to be suspicious of any stagnant convictions when confronting the mysteries of the human mind, one enabled to probe the most intriguing mysteries lying concealed in the complex operations of the evolving human consciousness, one adding new discoveries, and one awakening humanity to ever greater mysteries. I ask that I be a pioneer in the works of human behavior, that I have the audacity to be relentless in the quest, and have the quiet resolve to become one of the greatest and most elucidating cultural forces in the fields of chiropractic, psychology, philosophy, and theology. I ask that I am enabled to further develop my revolutionary psycho-transformative tool with a thousand uses called The Quantum Collapse Process, and that I am able to live a privileged and high-cultured life for the sake of fulfilling this lifelong quest.

Words of Wisdom and Power

- *I am a star; my destiny is to shine.*
- *I am a master of details, and I see my path clearly.*
- *I am the author of my life.*
- *Whoever has the most certainty, rules.*
- *The truth of me is light.*
- *God is the power, I'm the vision; we're the team.*

Chapter Eleven

Materialization: The Blueprint of Creation

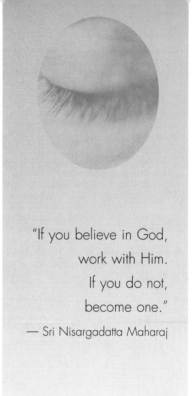

"If you believe in God, work with Him. If you do not, become one."

— Sri Nisargadatta Maharaj

Y ou have a purpose here on Earth. Your purpose is clear when you're guided by your soul, and clouded when you're distracted by the many personas you have. Every time you complete The Quantum Collapse Process, you dissolve personas, empower your true being, and clarify your inspiring purpose. Your purpose is the "why" that draws to you the "hows" in order for your "whats" to come true.

Have you ever gone to a seminar and learned a new set of skills? You received a great new list, a whole bundle of hows, but for some reason you just didn't apply them. The ratio between what you know and how much you actually do is determined by the size of your why. You can learn everything it takes to get your goal, but if your why is too small, you won't do what it takes. If your why is big enough, you'll learn something and then begin doing it; the hows will take care of themselves. But without a meaningful why, little will happen.

People have asked me, "John, how is it that you've stayed focused on your objective for 29 years?" I tell them it's simply because I have a big enough why. I was given a clear vision and message and got a big enough why to do what I'm here for. That's what motivates us and keeps us all going.

There are many levels of excuse in answer to the question, "Why aren't you self-actualizing your life and living exactly the way you would love it to be?" and they're all based on fears and forms of guilt.

I haven't self-actualized my life because . . .

- I *desire to* lose the fat on my body first.
- I *want to* pay off my debts first.
- I *need to* complete my education first.
- I *ought to* spend time doing charity work at my church first.
- I *have to* raise my family first.

None of those are necessarily true. They're all excuses for not doing what you love, but excuses won't bring you your dreams. If a person was absolutely certain and had an unshakable belief in themselves and what they do, you could take away their money and everything they have and they'd just create it again. To materialize your dreams, you must consistently take two wise action steps:

1. *Define your dreams.* If you don't define them, don't expect to have them.

2. *Ask yourself what's in the way of those dreams.* It makes a difference. If you find yourself making excuses, know that *any* excuse can be dissolved by a Collapse. Procrastination, which I define as putting off living your dreams, is based primarily on three things: an un-chunked and un-detailed goal, a lopsided perception, and a dream that isn't linked or aligned with your highest values or

purpose. Break any goal into doable steps, balance your perceptions, and link your dreams to your highest values, and you'll break through procrastination and act. Self-actualization requires no excuses, but people use excuses to justify why they're not doing what they would love to do.

I've been working with doctors for about 20 years, buying and selling practices and training and consulting with them. I could take a doctor who's been seeing 500 patients a week and move them to a tiny clinic in some little town, and within a matter of a months, they'd be back up to 500 patients a week. But I could take somebody else whose mentality is 50 patients a week and sell them a 500-patients-a-week practice, and in a few months, it would be down to 50 patients a week.

This phenomenon is the result of a vibrational state of consciousness that has little or nothing to do with the outer world and everything to do with your own inner world. What lessens the power of your inner world are your exaggerated and minimized perceptions in the seven areas of your life. Those are the fears and forms of guilt behind your self-limitation. The Breakthrough Experience is about dissolving the lopsided perceptions in the seven areas of life and freeing up your spirit to soar and fulfill.

I was once a special guest speaker at a dental conference in Texas on the topic of temporomandibular joint (TMJ) disorder. I was a young professional student at the Texas Chiropractic College at the time, but I was lecturing to dentists because I'd studied extensively on this subject. I arrived at the conference and discovered that the only available place to sit was with the dental nurses.

Seeing the portable demonstration table I had brought with me for my presentation, one of the nurses asked me, "Why are you here at the convention?"

I said, "I've come here to speak."

"What are you going to speak on? Are you a doctor?"

"No, I'm in the process of becoming one."

Some of the dental nurses looked puzzled. I guess I didn't fit their belief system about a doctor. My age and youthful look threw them. Isn't it amazing how we exaggerate or minimize our perceptions?

Do you know what the average doctor reads during their studies? More than 80 books. What do you call the person who graduates at the very bottom of the class? Doctor. But study and absorb 80 textbooks, and you've read the necessary material to become a doctor. By doubling that and studying 150 books on dentistry, you can be at the cutting edge of the industry, one of the noted specialists in the world ready to lecture on TMJ. I proved that to myself because I did exactly that. The dentists I spoke to didn't know any better once I began speaking. They just assumed I was a dental specialist because I was abreast of the newest TMJ information. I was supposed to speak for 30 minutes, but once I got going, they extended my time to nearly four hours. With less fear and guilt, almost anything can become possible. My dream was to teach, and my dream was becoming fulfilled.

The nurses imagined doctors as being above them; that's why they put themselves down and worked for the doctors. If those same nurses were to see their doctors as a reflection of themselves, they'd say, "Oh, I have the makings of a doctor, too." The value and prestige of entire professions has a lot to do with their collective self-image.

The same principle applies to you in relation to anybody you admire or think is above you. Your affirmation here could be, "If they can do it, I can do it!" You've got whatever they have, in your own form, and the only difference is that they're expressing it one way and you're expressing it in another. Collapse them and those qualities that you admire. You'll find yourself spontaneously starting to manifest what you thought you didn't have.

I simply had learned that if you intensely studied 30 minutes a day on the topic you have chosen to master, you could be at the cutting edge of your field at the end of seven years. If you studied 60 minutes a day on the topic you have chosen to master, you could be at the cutting edge of your field at the end of about four years. If you studied 120 minutes a day on the topic you have chosen to master, you could be at the cutting edge of your field in three years. And if you studied 180-plus minutes a day on the topic you have chosen to master, you could be at the cutting edge of your field at the end of two years. Dentistry was just one of many subjects I committed to understanding and mastering. Once you understand the truth of reflective consciousness and you follow a simple strategy, the sky becomes your limit.

Being, Doing, and Having

You are here to fulfill a mission. Your mission has three components: your states of being, doing, and having. If you don't identify what you would love to have and be in your life, just like what you would love to do in your life, the universe is likely to give you something entirely unpredictable. When you enter a country, you must declare your "goods"; and when you come into your body, you must declare what you would love out of life. The more you declare and ask for, the more fulfillment you can receive.

Tell me what you do and what you have, and I'll tell you a lot about who you are. If you have a lot of clients, businesses, wealth, and resources and you do a lot of service, you'll be labeled a "somebody." But if you do nothing and have nothing, society labels you a "nobody." When people do great service and have massive resources and really make a difference in the world, others automatically go, "Wow!"

Attendants in The Breakthrough Experience sometimes say, "No, I'm above all that. I don't look at what people do or have to determine who they are; I don't label them that way." But if somebody significant who has and does a lot stands next to them, they visibly wilt and crumple with self-incrimination. If a multibillionaire or someone extremely beautiful or absolutely brilliant comes into the room, they're intimidated. It's our nature to grow and expand our consciousness and outstretch every quality of our lives. Anyone who doesn't self-destructs because they're not fulfilling their divine purpose of continued evolvement, expansion, and awakening.

Because there's an inherently balancing mixture of be, do, and have, every time you try to *get* something for nothing or *give* something for nothing, you temporarily stagnate your true self-worth and cloud the clarity of your mission. This form of disequilibrium is called *unfair exchange*. This may sound a little shocking, but "giving" is something of a myth, for it can't be done without receiving. The widespread belief that we should all be giving persons is absolute nonsense. The master recognizes and transcends the myth of giving by knowing it's simply a form of exchange and transformation. The master understands fair exchange and knows that there's no giving without receiving in exact equilibrium.

Do you know people who think they're purely giving, charity-oriented altruists? If somebody says, "I would love to give this to you from my heart; I love to give, it's my nature," you can test for their hidden agenda by saying, "Oh, thank you so much for this lovely gift," and then give it to someone else right then and there, or possibly ignite it in front of them. Suddenly their hidden agenda surfaces, and the expectation behind their giving is revealed.

If they had truly given for the sake of giving, they would be able to appreciate your action. But if the hidden agenda is, "You're supposed to appreciate my exquisite taste, thank me, and be grateful," it will suddenly leap up and they'll react. Know that giving and taking maintain equilibrium. Become awakened to others and your own hidden agendas.

Presence is an important key to self-mastery. You cannot be

present if you perceive yourself as giving something for nothing, or getting something for nothing. A way to maintain presence is simultaneous fair exchange. So self-mastered people maintain fair exchange in their lives. That's why one of the most ancient Greek proverbs said, "Payment is due when services are rendered." That's remaining *present*. At the exact moment services are rendered, payment is made. When you're out of exchange, you block presence.

Have you ever owed something to someone and felt guilty and fearful for months or years? It ran around in your mind and you didn't have a clear consciousness because you felt out of fair exchange. Anytime you feel out of exchange in any of the seven areas of life— spiritual, mental, vocational, financial, social, familial, physical—you go out of presence and generate fear and guilt, and you will hold yourself back until you bring it perceptually back into fair exchange.

Fair exchange isn't limited to physical items; it's also about a mind game. If you receive a large inheritance and you don't know what you've done to deserve it, some equilibrating force is likely to reduce that amount to exactly what you feel you've earned. You might spend it, lose it in investments, or use it for sudden illness, desperate friends, or acute emergencies. To equilibrate your perception and feel that there has been fair exchange, you'd be wise to find out what you did to earn what you have received. The second you do, your mind becomes clear and present. When you feel you've earned it, you manage the money entirely differently. This is a very powerful principle, because we accumulate baggage every time we have imbalances in our perceptions and don't become aware of the equilibration.

What Is Your True Value?

Here's another twist to the principle: Until you value yourself, don't expect others to. The world around you reflects the world within you. When you set a higher true value on your being, doing, and having, that's what you will receive.

Say you're an actor and you decide that your fee is x dollars, and somebody offers you a role for one-tenth that amount. If you take their offer, you're saying that your true value is one-tenth the amount you originally set. You dilute your value in the marketplace. But if a lower offer comes in and you own your true value, saying, "No, it's this amount; that's my value," you'll get it. By owning it, I don't mean with your exaggerating, self-righteous persona; I mean your true centered being. Then you're in fair exchange and your self-worth grows. Otherwise, you feel out of exchange, like you did something for nothing, which lowers or dilutes your true self-worth and lowers the other person's accountability, responsibility, and eventual dignity.

"I ask for what I want; they pay it. It's that simple."
— Harrison Ford

Have you ever felt that you deserved more for something you'd done, but didn't demand it, and felt devalued afterwards? I consulted with a doctor in Europe a few years ago who was devaluing her services and charging very little. I said to her, "Go back to your practice and raise your fee. Charge a professional fee, and you'll get quality clients."

She went back to her office, and although she was frightened, she knew she wasn't in fair exchange. She'd been giving a special deal to one client for four years. She finally admitted that she resented him; she didn't want him to come to her office. She was frustrated, and her staff didn't want to have to deal with him either. After four years of giving this person her services for less than half price, thinking she was doing it out of kindness but with a hidden agenda and anger, she finally confronted him.

She said, "I think we've been out of exchange. It would be wise for us, starting next month, for you to gradually approach the full fee."

He went ballistic! He cussed her out and screamed, "You're not worth it! There's no way I'd pay that much money to you." As he stormed out of the place, her staff gathered around her and hugged her and said, "Bravo! That should have been done years ago!"

Before we consulted, she was still in the myth that people liked her for undercharging them, but this man was resenting her and hiding it, and she was resenting herself and hiding it, too. She finally got back in fair exchange, and her business has now grown extensively compared to what it was before she got the courage to ask for what she truly deserved.

The universe is asking you, "What is your value?" and waiting patiently until you finally wake up to it.

Your Mission Statement

It's now time to write your life's mission statement. Maybe you remember Tom Cruise in the movie *Jerry Maguire* when he was writing a mission statement for his company. As you create your own statement, your objective can be similar. Scan back over what you wrote in your Love List, and from those dreams, compose a statement of purpose consisting of three sentences or paragraphs—one for each of the *be, do,* and *have* components. When you're done, you'll have a statement that looks something like this one written by a healer:

*"I _____, hereby declare before myself, others, and God, that my primary purpose in life is to **be** a master healer and teacher. I **do** this by continually learning and absorbing every form of healing known to humankind. I integrate and synthesize their essence and take the best of the best methods and procedures. I figure out how to serve people most efficiently and effectively in the shortest period of time. I **have** in return the opportunity to receive incredible*

financial and social compensation. In my pursuit of the universal laws of healing, I am enabled to travel the world, exploring ancient healing centers and meeting the most extraordinary professional healers known to man."

As you write, remember to include these key points:

1. Write something that inspires you. Include what you would love to *have* in fair exchange for what you would love to *do* so you'll be motivated to fulfill it.

2. Put your mission statement in the present tense rather than the future tense, and write it from your heart and soul. Let neither your self-righteous persona exaggerate it, nor your self-wrongeous persona minimize it.

3. Don't worry about whether you can manifest it right away. I'll give you the tools for that in the upcoming pages.

4. Don't disconnect from what you're presently being, doing, and having. Include a component of whatever you're doing today in service to the world. If there's a significant difference, make sure they're merged or linked in some way so you can make the transition from what you *are* doing to what you *will* be doing.

You mission statement will reflect the purpose you're willing to live, regardless of pleasure and pain, or whether people like or dislike you, own or disown you. It transcends concerns of success or failure. This is your moment to decide what you would love to dedicate your life to, so let's begin.

Writing Your Mission Statement

1. **Review your Love List,** while reflecting on its magnificence.

2. **Thank your soul** for revealing to you this previous Love List, and thank your soul in advance for revealing to you what you would love.

3. **Ask your soul what it would love for you to fulfill.** Ask your soul for your mission, purpose, calling, vision, or divine design; and tune in to what you would love to dedicate your life to, the mission that aligns with your highest values. You can use a prayer or affirmation request like this one to lift you into a more illuminated state and prepare you for receiving:

Dear Soul,

I ask that I may be worthy of receiving your divine revelation.
I ask that I may be receptive to your grace.
I ask that my heart be opened and the outline of my destiny be revealed.
I ask that I may be humbled by the truth you provide before me.
I ask that my destiny become revealed now through my writing.

4. **Write this revelation in the *be, do,* and *have* sequence below.**

I _____ hereby declare before myself, others and God that my primary purpose in life is to . . .

be_____

_____

_____

_____

_____

_____

do_____

_____

_____

_____

_____

have_____

_____

_____

_____

_____

When you wrote your mission statement, did you feel something in your heart? To the exact degree you wrote it truly from your open heart, that statement has a special, immortal vibration. It is your true calling and the reason you were put here on Earth.

You can refine your mission statement at any time. Whatever you put down is only a starting point. Do you realize that you could put it in your computer and keep refining it throughout the rest of your life? Mine started in 1972, and it has been refined and updated 44 times since then.

The Manifestation Formula

When you dedicate your life to fulfilling your purpose, and appreciate whatever comes on your journey, you'll be amazed at how quickly and dramatically your life changes. However, knowing your purpose is just the first step. What follows next is The Manifestation Formula, a ten-step process for taking your inspirations and making them real.

1. Clarify your purpose. The clearer your purpose, the greater your certainty and sense of direction in life, and the more likely you are to materialize your goals and dreams. Make it your goal to consistently read and refine your purpose. Put it on a computer, review it daily, and update it. Set out to make it a masterpiece. Sometimes I read a book or a story and get one sentence out of the entire text that brings tears to my eyes, and whenever that happens, I modify that sentence to fit my life and splice it into my updated mission statement. That's part of the inspiration. Look for sentences and ideas that bring grateful tears to your eyes, and enter them into your life's mission statement.

2. Link all seven areas of life to your purpose. Anything you regularly do that isn't linked to or aligned with your purpose becomes a distraction and a burden. Wisdom is the realization that every action is part of your purpose, and it's just waiting for you to discover its meaning and connection. One gentleman started using his time emptying the trash to exercise, meditate, visualize, set goals, and repeat his affirmations. Make a list of everything you do in a normal day, and ask yourself, "How does this help me fulfill my mission?" Keep writing until you can honestly say, "Thank God I get to do this!" When you love what you do, it takes you to what you love.

3. Think about what you would love. What do you think might happen if you took total command of your thoughts? That's why I asked you to write down your dreams, because by that very act, you start to think about them, and the more you concentrate on them, the faster the dreams and goals on your Love List materialize. Write your dreams down and think about them. Concentrate your thoughts on what you would love, and make it materialize. It *is* worth your time.

4. Visualize what you would love. The more detail you can envision, the more power you have. You are a co-creator, and the more vision and visualization you have, the greater your power to create. Imagine the finest details of what you would love to see. When I visualize a seminar, I see myself in a particular location with a certain number of people, and I imagine the ideas I'm going to share and what they're going to get out of it—everything I can think of. If your dream is to travel, cut out pictures of the places you want to go and design a mosaic. Visualize exactly how you want your travels to be, down to the most minute detail.

5. Affirm what you would love. What you say makes a great difference in your life, so what would you love to say to yourself? If you *knew* you couldn't fail, what would you say to yourself? If you had the opportunity to repeat three top priority statements or words of power, what would they be? Not whiny illusions such as, "I'm always happy and I'm never sad," but crystal-clear, powerful, and concise statements such as "Whoever I touch becomes healthy and inspired," or "I pay myself first, because I'm worth it," or "I am a master healer; my hands are gifted." The exercises at the end of this chapter will guide you in creating your own affirmations.

6. Feel what you would love. The four most powerful creative feelings are gratitude, love, inspiration, and enthusiasm. They give you the power to manifest your dreams, and they appear in your heart, mind, and body when you're in a state of equilibrium. The more vitality and energy you put into what you're doing, the greater the reward you get back; so put all four feelings into the writing and the reading of your Love List, mission statement, and affirmations.

7. Write what you would love. Writing down what you would love is the first step in translating intangible ideas into tangible realities. Writing or typing activates the kinesthetic areas of your brain and puts associations in the cerebral hemispheres, which activate and stimulate visual, auditory, and kinesthetic effects. The result is that you end up materializing what you write about, so write it down!

8. Act on what you would love. Do you sometimes feel inspired and get great ideas, but fail to act on them? Many people write down their goals and then fail to follow through because they don't simplify or "chunk them down" into simple steps they can easily complete. Ask yourself these Seven Quality Questions of Self-Actualization, and don't give up until you find the answers. Your objective is to make your avocation your vocation.

a.   What would I absolutely love to do in life?

b.   How do I become handsomely or beautifully paid to do it?

c.   What are the seven highest-priority action steps I could complete today that would enable me to begin doing what I love?

d.   What obstacles might I run into and how do I solve them in advance?

e.   What worked and didn't work today?

f.   How do I do what I would love more effectively and efficiently?

g. How did whatever I experienced today, whether positive or negative, serve me and my purpose?

These are extremely powerful questions, and your life will be transformed if you master and apply them.

9. Materialize what you would love. Meditating and concentrating your thoughts on exactly how you would love your life to be will assist you in materializing your goals and dreams. If you follow this Manifestation Formula, you can bring your Love List into reality. Place no limits on how the universal substance can help you bring your dreams about; just affirm that you're at the perfect place, at the perfect time, to meet the perfect people to fulfill the perfect dreams. If you begin to experience any doubt, fill your mind with high-priority thoughts, and take high-priority action steps. Fill your day with the things you love, and watch what happens.

10. Be thankful for what you would love. The final step of The Materialization Formula is the acknowledgment, appreciation, and reception of what you've created. When you're thankful, you can open your heart and access your Divine Source of inspiration. Do the following seven-step exercise upon awakening, before going to sleep, and anytime you want to change your emotional state to one of love, gratitude, inspiration, or enthusiasm.

a. Turn your head up 45 degrees.

b. Turn your eyes up another 45 degrees.

c. Close your eyelids loosely.

d. Begin inwardly thanking all the people who have helped you become who you are today.

e. Continue this thankfulness until your heart opens and you feel a state of unconditional love, tears come pouring forth, and you clearly see how all of these people played a magnificent role in your unfolding life.

f.   When your heart is open and your tears are flowing, ask your divine Soul for its guidance, wisdom, and message.

g.   Wait for this message that will come from the innermost recesses of your Soul-mind. When it comes to your consciousness, write it down and follow it.

By being thankful for what you are, have, and do, you pave the way for ever-expanding being, having, and doing. Just as you continue rewarding others when they appreciate your gifts, so, too, does the universe reward you when you appreciate its gifts.

The Materialization Formula is your blueprint for creating what you love. *Purpose* plus *thought* plus *vision* plus *affirmation* plus *feeling* plus *writing things down in space and time* plus *taking action with energy on matter* plus *being thankful,* manifests things. Dreams are just a matter of discipline; this formula makes dreams possible.

I've heard people say things such as, "It's going to take me two or three years to fulfill one of my dreams," but I say, so what? What else would you do with those years anyway?

"God, I wouldn't want to go through ten years of college to achieve that." But what else are you going to do with your time? And if you don't, in ten years, where else are you planning on being?

Some people say, "I want to do this, but if it doesn't happen, it must not be meant to be," as if it were only up to fate or God. Anytime you hear yourself saying that, it just means that you're not really committed. If you're really determined, you can make it "meant to be." Be willing to do whatever it takes. Allow nothing to stop you.

At the end of your life, you're going to be asking yourself, "Did I do everything I could with everything I was given? Did I use all of my talents to the fullest?" What do you want the answers to be?

Lake Success

I once knew a man who wanted to be a healer. He was a left-brained intellectual type who didn't believe in personal development or motivational seminars, and primarily attended more technically oriented courses. When he graduated and went out into the world to practice, he thought that his skill and knowledge alone would guarantee his success. So he hung out his shingle, tried to practice . . . and nobody came. He didn't realize that becoming successful meant that he also had to be a manager, a salesman, and an entrepreneur with a vision. For 11 years he practiced, and not for one single month did he ever have enough money to pay his bills without help from his wife's income as a schoolteacher. At times he wanted to commit suicide, and actually attempted it on more than one occasion.

One day I was speaking in Lake Success, New York, to about 400 doctors in a big hotel ballroom. I was 20 minutes into my presentation when the door at the back of the room opened, and in walked this gentleman. He was wearing a lime-green double-knit suit from the 1970s that made him look out of place among the well-dressed doctors there. He also looked skeptical, like he wasn't sure he belonged or even wanted to be there.

I spoke for another 20 minutes or so, talking about having a clear vision and being inspired about what you do. I don't know exactly what I said, but this gentleman suddenly moved up a few rows from the back of the room and began taking notes. After my first break, he came and sat in the fourth seat in the first row, right in front of me, and I could see then that he was a real country bumpkin-looking kind of guy. He was tall, thin, and awkward and didn't look very well off. But somehow what I was saying was touching him. He was now present and listening intently.

Toward the end of my second segment, I shared the story about the boy who had been in a coma for three years. It was one of the miraculous moments of my life when, right there in my office, in my *hands*, he had come out of his coma. As I told the story, that man in the first row began to cry, suddenly remembering why he wanted to be a doctor. He was crying so hard that he bent down over his knees with tears dripping from his eyes, nose, and mouth.

When I finished, a group of doctors came up and gave me hugs and had me sign my books and tapes. The man was still seated in the front row, in a kind of trance state. He finally came up to me, the last person remaining. He didn't say anything; he just put his arms around me and held me. He cried and cried, and finally said, "Thank you. I think you saved my life."

I had to get into a limousine and go on to another city to speak, but at 5 o'clock the following Monday, my assistant came to me and said, "Doctor, there's a gentleman on the phone who really, truly wants to speak with you." I picked up the receiver and said, "This is Dr. Demartini. How can I help you?"

He said, "I don't know if you remember me, but last Thursday I was in your class and gave you a hug at the end of the program. Dr. Demartini, I want to thank you. Do you have a moment for me to tell you a story?"

"Absolutely."

"I've wanted to kill myself three times in my life, and five or six days before your program, I almost did it. A friend of mine happened to find me in that low moment, and he said, "God bless it, don't you leave this earth before at least going out and trying to learn how to be successful. Your family deserves it and so do you. Get out of your head and go learn how to be a successful doctor. Get over this life that you're living.'"

The man then expressed to me that he took the only money that he and his wife had and came to my introductory seminar at Lake Success. He said, "When I got to the seminar, I pulled up to that magnificent hotel and saw all those Mercedes, BMWs, and Porsches in the parking lot. I felt so humiliated that I wanted to turn around and leave. But I decided to park in a corner of the lot way in the back where nobody could see me, and I slouched down in my car until everybody went in. As I waited, I saw people arriving that I'd gone to school with, and I was shaking with fear that they'd see me hiding there. Then when I walked in, I heard you talking about the 'cosmic AT&T system,' that what we think about is what we bring about, and I thought to myself, *This guy is exactly what I feared. This is a waste of time.*

"I was about to walk out when you said that I didn't pick my profession, God picked me, and I mustn't ever forget the moment I was called. Man, you knocked me so hard when you said that! At that moment, I flashed back to the real reason I wanted to be a doctor, and I'd forgotten it. All of a sudden, I felt that everybody else in the room was gone and I was there alone, and you were talking to me. I felt that everything you said you were saying to me. I wrote it all down, and I gave you a hug afterwards."

I said, "Yes, I remember that."

"You told me to think about the details of my dreams, to not let anything enter my mind except my dreams, so I pulled over in my old car. I got out a notepad and wrote down every single patient I wanted to see that I had forgotten; every single patient that I wanted to help; and all their subluxations, health problems, and children's names. I thought about their professions and their companies, about every detail I could imagine about them, and I spent the next seven hours memorizing people's names, just like you told me to do.

"You said that if I couldn't wait to see my patients, they couldn't wait to see me; if I became inspired about what I was doing, people would get inspired about it, too. When I got back, I didn't go home, I went to my office. You said that if I have a disorganized office and things are a mess, that nobody is going to want to be around it, because people are drawn to order, organization, and clarity. I went into my office and absolutely cleaned it spotlessly. I put everything in its proper place. I threw out anything that didn't serve me. I organized new patient files as if they were going to come, and I got my order and inspiration back.

"I spent Thursday night, Friday, Saturday, and Sunday morning in my office, meditating, organizing, thinking, and dreaming, because I didn't want to go home until I felt I was going to be a success. You told me that if I humbled myself to an Intelligence greater than myself, that miracles would happen, and by God, that's what I did. On Sunday morning, I said a prayer and asked for guidance. Then I went home and walked into my house and saw my wife there. I felt for the first time in 11 years that I deserved her. My wife turned, saw me, and embraced me. She said, 'Welcome home.' She knew something special had happened.

"That night I could barely sleep because I had so many patients running through my mind. I had my vision back, my clarity, my inspiration. I remembered why I was a doctor and why I was drawn into that profession. I remembered my dream when I first got into professional school and how much I wanted to serve people. I realized that I had been in my own way, and I was no longer going to let anything stop me from being a healer—nothing! I was going to be like Christ. I wanted to be able to touch them and bring about miracles, so I prayed for that spirit to guide me.

"Dr. Demartini, I wanted to call you because I just finished my first day back in practice. The most I ever saw in a single day in all those years was 18 patients. My average day was nine patients. I can't fully explain what happened today, but I saw 52 patients. People came out of the woodwork; they showed up from all over the place. So thank you for helping me renew my vision. Because, by God, I *am* a healer, and I'm not going to let anything stop me from that dream from now on."

I share that story because it relates in some degree to all of us. Every single person has a vision, an inspiration, and a gift inside. Everyone has a calling and a commitment and has the power of genius. But you must be willing to organize your life and let nothing stop you. If you have a dream, then carry it through the days of your life and don't let anything keep you from it—and you'll awaken your genius. You're not just your body, nor just a personality; you're a spiritual soul, and you have a vast destiny that neither you nor I can fully comprehend as yet.

"Salvation does not come through the sight of me.
It comes through discipline and hard work,
so work diligently for your own liberation."
— The Buddha

Some people wonder why I put so much information into my courses and books. Have you ever been to a seminar and realized that the presenter could have covered in one morning what they took two days to do, and the rest was filler? I made a commitment to give people more than they expected, to take them beyond their sphere of knowledge and open up new horizons. Therefore, I'm blitzing you. I'm assuming your intuition, study, and life have brought you to this point, and you're ready to go to a higher level of understanding and functioning. I don't treat you like a victim, but like a self-actualized individual, a genius who is ready to wake up to the great equilibrium and divine order that surrounds you. I do what teacher Marilyn Wilhelm did in this respect: I treat people as if they were geniuses, and that's what they become. I attempt to speak to the part of you that already knows all this and more, to wake it up and help it come forward to direct your life.

We just have one more step together on this journey, and the next chapter will bring together everything we've covered so far.

Exercise 1

What we say to ourselves impacts our lives. Affirmations absolutely do work, but not if you give up on them before they can begin to materialize. Create your own affirmations, and don't stop saying them for two years before deciding whether they worked or not.

When creating your affirmations:

- Use words in the present tense, not the future or past.

- Describe realities that are possible, not fantasies with impossible time frames.

- Don't use absolute statements such as "always" or "never."

- Use simple, powerful words joined into brief phrases.

- Use words that carry feelings of gratitude, love, inspiration, or enthusiasm.

- Use words that you're willing to say for life.

On the lines provided below (or on a separate piece of paper), write the ten most inspiring and meaningful "words of power" affirmations that you'd love to say to yourself multiple times daily for the rest of your life.

Examples:
"I am a genius, and I apply my wisdom."
"I am a master reader; whatever I read I retain."
"I am a master of persistence, and I do what it takes."
"I do what I love, and I love what I do."

1._____

_____

2._____

_____

3._____

_____

4._____

_____

5._____

_____

6._____

_____

7._____

_____

8._____

_____

9._____

_____

10._____

_____

Now record these words of power onto an audiocassette tape or CD. Say them clearly and with feeling. Have someone you respect also say them to you. Consider playing your favorite piece of music in the background while you do the taping.

Exercise 2

The following exercise will help you manifest your dreams by "chunking down" your goals or projects into doable action steps. The purpose is to break them down into bite-size pieces that you know you can manage, thus helping you overcome inertia, hesitation, and procrastination. When you clarify your vision in this way, you'll know that it's absolutely achievable. Remember the old adage: How do you eat an elephant? One bite at a time! A big project can be easily handled if you just chunk it down into small enough bites.

1.   In the first column, write down one of the goals from your Love List.

2.   In the second column, chunk your goal into small action steps by first asking yourself, "What are the seven highest priority action steps that would let me accomplish what I've written in Column 1?" Don't worry about whether you can do them or not. For example, if your goal was to become a multibillionaire and charitable philanthropist by age 40, your seven highest priority action steps might include opening a brokerage account, establishing a corporation, and identifying the charities you care about most. These are your "first generation" chunks.

3.   In the third column, you'll chunk the items from Column 2 even further by asking the same question again: "What are the seven highest priority action steps that, if I were to do them, regardless of whether I think I can, would let me accomplish what I have written in Column 2?" For example, you might chunk "Open a brokerage account"

down to "Ask my successful friend Andy who his broker is; schedule an appointment; prepare a list of questions to take to the meeting," and so on. Again, write seven action steps for each item you listed in Column 2. These are your "second-generation" chunks.

4. If necessary, keep chunking these 49 action steps down through further generations. The idea is to chunk down until you come up with a list of action steps that are so small, you can say without hesitation that you can now do them.

Objective from my Love List that I would love to manifest	First generation of seven high-priority action steps	Second generation of seven high-priority action steps
_____	_____	_____
		_____
		_____
		_____
		_____
		_____
		_____
	_____	_____
		_____
		_____
		_____
		_____
		_____
		_____
	_____	_____
		_____
		_____
		_____
		_____
		_____
		_____
	_____	_____
		_____
		_____
		_____
		_____
		_____
		_____
	_____	_____
		_____
		_____
		_____
		_____
		_____
		_____
	_____	_____
		_____
		_____
		_____
		_____

Exercise 3

If you wrote down the seven highest-priority action steps you could do every day to help you live your mission, and did it every day for two years, at the end of that time you'd have more than 700 pages. By then you'd find a pattern to your priorities. That pattern would show you the top actions, the priorities of your priorities, to help you become most effective and efficient in whatever it is you would love to do. You could try it for a month, but the longer you go, the more your certainty grows. This is a real gem—if you do it.

By completing this exercise, I learned that the four things I do most powerfully are research, write, travel, and speak. When I do them, every one of my dreams starts manifesting. You must find your own. There's no right or wrong about your priorities, and no one's priorities are better or worse. They simply reflect your individual values. Once you identify and stick to your priorities, the rest of your life seems to just fall into place. So just do it. Every day, and every moment of your life, counts.

Review your Love List and mission statement, and ask yourself this question: What are the seven highest-priority action steps I can do *today* that will help me live my mission or fulfill my purpose in life?

#1 _____

_____

#2 _____

_____

#3 _____

_____

#4 _____

_____

#5 _____

_____

#6 _____

_____

#7 _____

_____

Two additional high-priority actions I found invaluable in my life was the logging of all of my most significant achievements, and blessings. Whenever you achieve one of the more important goals on your Love List, be sure to record it. Periodically reviewing what you have accomplished can be motivating and can help you build greater confidence. Whenever you experience any significant blessing in life, be sure to also record it. Periodically reviewing your blessings can be inspiring and can help you grow in gratitude. I have both logs reaching far back into my life. They certainly keep me going.

Words of Wisdom and Power

- *What would I love to do?*
- *If they can do it, I can do it.*
- *I maintain fair exchange in everything I do.*
- *I set a value on my time and life, and I receive what I set.*
- *I fill my life with high-priority actions because time is precious.*
- *Did I do everything I could, with everything I was given?*

Chapter Twelve

Completion: Full Circle

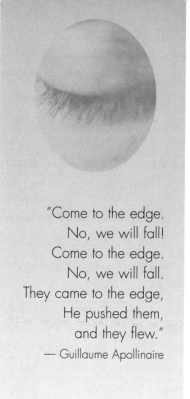

"Come to the edge.
No, we will fall!
Come to the edge.
No, we will fall.
They came to the edge,
He pushed them,
and they flew."

— Guillaume Apollinaire

When Paul Bragg helped me awaken my vision, I was frightened because there seemed to be no way I could fulfill it. I was an illiterate surfer . . . what made me think I could ever be a teacher? It was incongruent, but the vision was clear, so when he gave me my affirmation about being a genius, I stuck to it.

Bragg said, "Your mind dictates your destiny, and your dominant thought determines your world. Don't just repeat the words I've given you; *become* them. Say them as if your life depended on them!" So I did, and when my friends in the tent mocked me, I just said them inside even more strongly.

When I look back on my life, I see that every moment has served me in what I'm presently doing. It has all been in perfect order. You, too, have experienced exact perfection for your destiny. Every single positive and negative experience or event has guided or pointed you along your way, and in the direction of your mission. That's why it's so important to awaken to your purpose and to Collapse any illusions distracting you from being grateful for your life. That's where certainty comes from. Everything that ever happened to you was perfect, and the day you realize that is the day you'll know what philosopher Gottfried W. Leibniz saw when he wrote about divine perfection. That's the day your genius will be reborn, and you'll begin leaving your immortal mark.

I'm a Genius, and I Apply My Wisdom

One time when I was speaking to about 1,500 doctors of chiropractic in Las Vegas, someone asked, "Will you share that story about how you became a healer?" The audience was made up predominantly of healers, and they wanted to reconnect to their core vision. A man and woman were sitting in the sixth or seventh row, where I could see them. As I began to tell the story, the couple's 16-year-old son, who wasn't interested in the class, entered the room. He'd been playing video games and ran out of money, so he came in and asked his mom for more coins, but she just said, "Sit down. *Ssshhh.* Just sit down." The young man rolled his eyes and sat down, looking bored and a bit pissed off.

As I told the story of what happened to me when I was 17, he suddenly looked at me and zeroed in, because he could relate to it. When I said that someday when I'm 93, I want to share the same message with some 17-year-old that Paul Bragg shared with me, I knew that a part of him was thinking, *God, I wish I could be that young man.* Because I had touched his heart, he was in tears when I finished. At the end of my talk, people came up to me, and I didn't see the young man again.

I spoke in Dallas about two months later, and there were the mother, the father, and the son, right in the center of the front row. The mother asked if they could share a story with me, and I said, "Sure."

She said, "You couldn't possibly understand what's happened in our lives since we first heard your story, Dr. Demartini." She started crying, hugged her husband next to her, and continued, "I'm back in college. I'm a genius, and I apply my wisdom."

The husband came over to me and gave me a big hug, but he couldn't speak. He waved his hand and brought his son over, and the young boy said, "I'm a genius, and I apply my wisdom. I was at your class in Las Vegas, and you really moved me. You said that when you were 93, you wanted to have a 17-year-old to share with, and I really wanted to be him, but it wasn't possible because I couldn't be that age when you were 93. But then all of a sudden, after saying, *I'm a genius, and I apply my wisdom*, something happened to me. A great idea popped into my head. I realized it was 1993. And I'm 17," and he asked if there was any way that he could be the 17-year-old boy in 1993.

When he said that, tears just welled up in my eyes. I pulled out one of my business cards and asked him to write on the back the affirmation, *I'm a genius, and I apply my wisdom;* the year 1993; his name; and the city, state, and country he was from. I still carry it with me to this day.

Once the father regained his composure enough to speak, he said, "Seventeen years ago, I was blessed with the birth of my son," and he choked up a little, and his wife held him until he could continue. "I asked God that if it was his will to bring me a son who could be a great chiropractor, I would do whatever it takes to make that possible." He even named the child B.J., after one of the most famous chiropractors in the world. He didn't want to influence his son, or force him to be anything, but if it were possible, that was his dream. He said that for 16 years, his son showed little interest in becoming a chiropractor.

"And then one day at your talk, by God's will our son was there. You got us all saying, 'I'm a genius, and I apply my wisdom.' You impacted him like nothing else did before, and he decided shortly afterwards. He put his arms around me and said, 'Dad, I've decided to be a chiropractor.'" At the moment his son told him his decision, the father said to himself, "Thank you, God. Thank you for fulfilling a dream I've waited 16 years for."

There was a mixture of fate, destiny, human will, and divine design all in that moment. We were standing there together in a small circle, and all of us just embraced with gratitude, love, and inspiration.

B.J. has now finished chiropractic college and has gone into practice with his father. Today they have a very successful practice, and . . . B.J.'s mother finished her education.

Passing the Torch

That experience with B.J. is what Paul Bragg gave to me. It's called "passing the torch." If you have only one of those moments in life, your life is worthwhile. If you dedicate your life to having a hundred, or a thousand, or a million of them, that's worth getting up for every morning. It becomes your target, through thick and thin, through energy or exhaustion, through happiness or sadness, to do what you love and what you've dreamed of.

I'm a teacher, healer, and philosopher who studies universal laws as they relate to body, mind, and spirit, particularly as they relate to healing. I'm here to travel around the world and do whatever it takes, travel whatever distance, and pay whatever price to share my services of love. That's it. That's what I do. When you find your own unique cause—or re-find it, because sometimes you forget it—then you have the gift of life. That's what life is, something inspiring that you can dedicate your energies to. The quality of your life is directly proportionate to your feeling of productivity and to the service you bring to this world.

Sharing love, wisdom, and healing is one of my most fulfilling and inspiring actions. It's the fulfillment of my dream and mission. I've embraced both the pain and pleasure that accompany it, and my rewards have been exactly proportionate. Each weekend at The Breakthrough Experience somebody experiences a profound Collapse and opens their heart to their life's magnificence. How could my vision not become fueled by such regular blessings?

Ancient wisdom dictates that if you don't pass or light another torch, you won't receive greater light. Whatever you would love to master, pass it on like a torch. If you help others achieve what they would love to achieve in life, you'll be more enabled to achieve what *you* would love. If you would love to be a teacher, then teach. If you would love to be an actor, then act and help others learn to act. If you would love to be a writer, sit down and begin writing and help others do the same. Whatever you would love to be, do, or have, make a commitment to serve others with your skill, and you'll draw the people to fit your niche and help you grow.

Another part of self-mastery is knowing when to speak and when to remain silent. To those who believe, no proof is necessary. To those who don't, no proof is possible. Waste no words on those who seek not. Sometimes silence is more powerful than speech. Be wise in your selection of torch carriers.

When you share your inspirations and let them rub off on others who are ready to hear, they share them in turn, and as your message rolls downhill, you receive more inspiration, enthusiasm, and light. The quicker you gather information and the faster you give to others what you've learned, the more you remember. The more time that elapses between receiving and broadcasting, the less you retain and the less certain you become. If you'd love to have a photographic mind, immediately give out what you've taken in. Acknowledge your natural mentor as well as your natural student, and maximize your own evolution.

Illusions Also Serve

On your destiny path, you'll pass through many domains of existence. As you grow in body, mind, and spirit and pass through these concentric spheres of consciousness or phases of life, you'll break through many illusions. Remember how in elementary school, above the blackboard they had pictures of little balls that were meant to represent atoms? When you saw them, you probably thought, *Oh, atoms are spheres;* but when you got into high school, you found out that they weren't exactly spheres after all and were made up of subatomic protons, neutrons, and electrons.

When you got to college, you found out that atoms are actually believed to be probability distributions of waves and particles; and that protons are made of quarks, gluons, and other subatomic particles. Then when you went on to receive your Ph.D., you discovered that that explanation was just a hypothesis, a theory that's still open to discussion. Now as a professor emeritus, you realize that all these theories are just somebody's belief systems. In some cases, they're nothing more than institutional imperatives, not truths, and anyone can come along with a new model and theory that will supersede them someday. Every once-believed truth eventually becomes another illusion on the next level of understanding.

If you were ten years old and I gave you $10, you'd be pretty happy; and if someone stole $10 from your piggy bank, you'd be pretty sad. If you were 20 years old and I gave you $100, you'd be happy; and if I took $100 away, you'd be sad. When you're 30 years old, receiving $1,000 makes you happy, and losing it saddens you. If you're 40 years old and I give you $10,000, you'd be pretty happy, and if I took $10,000 away, you'd be pretty angry. At age 50, if I were to write you a check right now for $100,000, that would probably elate you, and taking it away would depress you. And if you keep growing in wealth, by the age of 60, giving or taking $1,000,000 would make you happy or sad.

But if I were to give you $10 at 60, would I make you happy? Probably not. And taking $10 away wouldn't do a whole lot to a 60-year-old either. Each of those ages is at a different concentric sphere of wealth consciousness. Someone can run you at 10 years old with $10, but to get the same emotional reaction from a 60-year-old, you have to give or take away $1,000,000 because their perceived value has grown and they've evolved.

Everything is relative. The dollar numbers don't actually matter because gain and loss are just a matter of perception. Pleasure and pain, and elation and depression, are conserved through every moment and level of life. They keep growing in magnitude or multitude, but because you've also grown, these two imposters will feel exactly the same to you. Whatever makes you happy will make you sad to the same degree. Life doesn't really get any harder or easier than it already is—birth to the baby, kindergarten to the infant, dating to the adolescent . . . work, marriage, career, midlife crisis, aging, death, and whatever comes next—all are equal to the person experiencing them.

We don't experience challenges that are beyond us. Primary school students aren't given calculus. The whole world is a school, and it's the illusions of gain and loss, and fear and courage that makes it exciting and depressing, ideal and real, and ultimately fulfilling. At every level or sphere of life, there's a gratitude-based heaven or an ingratitude-based hell, depending on your perceptions at that moment. No matter how many levels you go through, you're going to remain in balance.

We go through an infinite series of concentric spheres, from judgment to indifference and then love, over and over again in a cycle. We're not here to be one-sided, we're not even here to be happy— we're here to love. Love is so much more profound than happiness. Happiness is but a transient emotion compared to the eternal truth, fulfillment, grandeur, and grace of love. And we're not meant to stay happy anyway. We're here to grow from quantum to quantum through love. The second we love one elusive quantum, we go to the next; and when we love that elusive quantum, we go on to still the next.

The masses are easily swayed by emotions and rhetoric. But as they individually evolve and become masterful, they join the fewer in number and greater in consciousness. They join with those who are guided by love and wisdom. It's not right or wrong that this happens; it's just the way it is. We have many people who play sports, but few top athletes; many painters, but few master artists; many who can carry a tune, but few musical geniuses. The truth has never been in the hands of the masses; it has always been in the hands of the *masters* in every field. Most people don't even want to know the truth; it scares them, and they'd rather have the comfort of their illusions. Why? Because the truth requires perfect accountability for one's own perceptions and lies, and some people aren't ready for that.

As you mature, you grow in wisdom, outreach, and accountability by facing and embracing your illusions. It's as if you're in the video game "Pac-Man," growing by consuming your illusions and turning them into love and wisdom. It happens in every area of life, and you wouldn't want it to ever stop. Life involves an infinite progression, and you're never done. If you think you're supposed to get someplace where it's all over, you've just "finited" the infinite and missed the big picture. I wouldn't love life to get easier; I'd love life to get more challenging, because the more challenge and chaos I perceive I've been given, the more order I'm able to create. I'd rather embrace life in its profoundness. I prefer that when I'm 100 years old, I'm taking on even more accountability than I do today. If I am, I'm still alive. If I'm not, I died long before my bodily death.

The Truth about Therapists

Both love and emotions are feelings, but love is a truth, and emotions are lies. If someone perceives an event to be more negative than positive and feels hurt by it, and if you say to them, "Oh, you poor thing; you're hurt, you're suffering," some people will call that compassion. But in many cases, what you may actually be doing is supporting their victimhood and helping them weaken themselves. This can stagger their growth by detouring them from the accountability for their own cause and effect and by sidetracking them from the recognition of the truth of equilibrium and The Great Discovery. I don't encourage that, because true love doesn't rescue illusions or support myths. If anything, it challenges them and equilibrates these lopsided illusions for the sake of truth.

> *"Do not seek to follow in the footsteps*
> *of the wise men of old. Seek what they sought."*
> — Matsuo Munefusa ("Basho")

People who say, "I was beaten, I was abandoned, I was hurt; I was this, that, and the other," are often looking for sympathy and compassion. They surround themselves with a support group that gives them this so-called compassion, and they stay stuck for years in some cases. Sometimes they don't get past it at all during their physical life.

Then the psychologist comes along and says, "Yes, you're a victim all right. *You're* innocent, and *they're* terrible for doing that to you," thereby disassociating their clients from their own cause and effect.

No therapy can be complete until cause and effect are one in space-time. So I come along and ask, "All right, where's the pleasure? How did it serve you? What were the benefits? Where have you done it yourself?" and neutralize and equilibrate the imbalanced charge. I find out how it served them and they're liberated. They realize that the person that they first thought victimized them was their helper and teacher, and there was nobody victimized in the first place.

A middle-aged gentleman came to The Breakthrough Experience in Houston years ago, and as far as he was concerned, there was absolutely nothing good about his father. He wrote down 90 negatives and no positives on The Quantum Collapse Process form. Since I thought it would be a great opportunity for everyone else to learn, I spent almost three hours working with him. If they could see how difficult yet possible it was for him to reach an openhearted state of love, the whole room might be motivated to open their hearts.

I sat with him one-on-one and kept persuading him to look deeper, again and again. I didn't make up or compel him to write anything he didn't really see, I just kept suggesting different angles and ways of looking at his father to find some benefits. Eventually he started to discover them. He finally saw the balance, how he'd done everything he'd accused his father of, how it had served him, and how his father had the opposite traits, also. Upon reaching equilibrium and attaining pure reflective consciousness, he opened up his heart to his father. At that instant, his dad appeared in his mind and he felt his presence. He opened up his heart and felt love for his father for the first time he could remember in his entire life.

Love had been sitting in his heart the whole time, but he had worn a facade or mask on top of that heart. It was a lie he carried around, and it covered up his love. When he finally took the mask away, he revealed an unbelievable love for his father. His face lost five years, he softened, his energy was transformed, and he became part of the team of attendees.

He left the seminar a changed man on Sunday night, but saw his psychiatrist on Monday and told her, "I went to a seminar this weekend and learned something very profound. I realized how much I love my father deep down inside, and how much he served my life."

He'd been seeing this therapist for 11 years and had developed a dependency dynamic with her. She said, "You just lost 11 years' worth of my therapy! You've gone into denial about what your father did, you were a victim, and now you can't even see that anymore. If I were you, I'd go to this Demartini guy and get your money back, and make him pay for the rest of your therapy with me until we get this thing resolved and back under control."

Now that's marketing! He called me on the phone, shaking with fear, caught in turmoil about losing his therapist. He had no attachment to me. He had experienced undeniable love for his father, but now he might be about to lose his 11-year security blanket, the psychiatrist. He said, "Dr. Demartini, I don't know how to say this, but I have to ask you for my money back. My psychiatrist said you brainwashed me. She said you've destroyed 11 years' worth of her work and should be paying for the rest of my therapy with her."

I said, "Wouldn't that be convenient for her? I love that marketing tool. I won't do that, but I'll tell you what I will do. If you can truly and honestly say, from your heart, that I didn't serve you in this program, you can have your money back. But if you ever decide that you're ready to go beyond the illusion your psychiatrist is attempting to promote and impose on you, and you want to return, just know that you'll have to repay it before coming to the next program. This door will always remain open for you, but you don't get something for nothing.

"You know as well as I do that yesterday you had love for your father. My advice is to not ever forget that. If she tries to impose on you the belief that he was a mean bastard and a son of a bitch, just know inside your heart that it's not ultimately true. For he is still your father with two sides, the perfect balance to your mother. To not love your own parents can take its toll on your life and well-being. It can even affect your heart if you try to fall back into your past angered illusion. Become aware of co-dependent relationships between you and your psychiatrist. Maybe if you take the time to Collapse her, you might be able to set her free."

Be aware that sometimes therapists are caught in areas of their own life where they haven't gotten past an issue. To work through their own charged illusions, they attract as clients the parts of themselves they have yet to love. They often put together support teams to justify these illusions. There are gradations of service providers in the mental health field, and they are at many different levels of awareness. Some are in victim modes about issues they haven't broken through, and some are very aware and enlightened.

As you go through the psychological development process, you may move from one therapist or analyst to another until you finally find one who understands cause and effect and is willing to awaken you to your magnificence and illumination. There are definitely therapists who are awakened, self-actualized beings, but until you're ready, you probably won't run into them or recognize them.

Some people mimic their therapists or religious teachers without thinking for themselves. When confronted, they either avoid the issue or parrot some more lines of generally misunderstood teaching. People who aren't willing to embrace the wisdom of their soul often copy other people they've given authority to. This won't create awakening or self-actualization immediately or directly. It's simply a way station on the road to illumination.

The Quantum Collapse Process doesn't require a therapist. Once it's understood and mastered, it doesn't always take hours of grueling soul-searching; it can take as little as an hour. It doesn't always take two pages; in some cases, it can be completed in a page or a few lines—that is, if you've narrowed your focus down to the priority issues.

I was doing a Collapse on my mother one time on a jet, and all it took was five lines. I cried tears of gratitude for my mother and saw a magnificent aspect about her that I'd never seen before. A wonderful elderly lady about my mother's age was sitting next to me. As I completed my few lines of the Collapse, I turned and looked at her with tears in my eyes. She began crying, too. I told this woman what I wanted to tell my mother. She in turn told me what she wanted to tell her son, and we embraced on that plane. I closed my eyes and cried and held her and told her what I felt. When I finally opened my eyes, people all around us were wiping tears from their eyes and looking for tissues. That lady had never met me before, but we held hands for the rest of the flight.

The man on my other side looked at me as if I was totally weird. He knew that the lady and I were total strangers; I think he was afraid I was going to hug him next!

You can do The Quantum Collapse Process anywhere. When you complete it, you fearlessly go so far past any form of self-consciousness that you're able to unveil the light of your true being. This extends out beyond your normal limiting personas. The truth really does set you free, and the power of your open heart will affect the people around you.

Identity Crisis

You need to know that The Breakthrough Experience won't make you happy. It's about something far beyond happiness and sadness. Every time you go from one concentric sphere of existence to another, every time you make a quantum leap to a new and different level of consciousness, you undergo a temporary identity crisis. This phenomenon is absolutely essential to growth, and the bigger the leap, the bigger the crisis. Your life is modeled on a belief and a perceptual system, and when you suddenly don't fit into that system anymore, when you've grown beyond it, you go through an identity crisis phase while you adapt to your new concentric model.

Picture an atom; it has positive protons in the core, and negative electrons in the surrounding shells. If you strip away an electron, the atom becomes more positive; and if you add an electron, it becomes more negative. Every time you add or subtract an electron, you change the charge of the atom. As humans, our charges are called "emotions," "belief systems," and "values." When you change the charge of an atom, it reacts differently to all the other atoms, and human beings are the same. We react differently to the world according to our old and new charges.

Anytime you strip away a belief system about good and evil, you're going to react differently to your life. You're so used to reacting in habitual ways that you'll think, *Hey, wait a minute! I can't behave in the old way, but I'm not really sure what I think about this now*, and *that* is the identity crisis. Stripping charges from an atom can actually create a different reacting element. In the same way, it creates a different person, and that is both painful and pleasurable. There is pleasure in your new freedom of relating, and pain due to the uncertainty of the new dynamic and the reactions of others.

Growth demands this. You must go through some degree of an identity crisis to grow. In fact, your whole life has been filled with a series of identity crises or periods of chaos; you're constantly shedding and renewing. Having identity crises is exactly where you want to live, though, because maximum growth occurs at the border of chaos and order. Without identity crises, you're stagnant.

If someone says to me, "I came to your seminar and I felt a little bit disoriented for part of a day," I say to them, "Great. That's exactly what was intended. It means that the seminar has changed your life. You're going through the normal identity crisis that's essential for your growth. You came seeking change, and you received it."

Nobody comes to a seminar thinking, *I want to be exactly the same when I walk out as when I came in*, because that's not the wisest use of time, energy, and money. In order to grow, you must make a change, and with change comes an identity crisis that's really the breaking through of old values and character habits.

When neophytes on the path of spiritual awareness and growth experience normal identity crises, they tend to look outside themselves for the cause and effect. The master looks within. Your own perceptions create your order or chaos. If you ever find yourself being overwhelmed during an identity crisis by too many new, lopsided perceptions, stop and Collapse them and the crisis will dissolve into presence. I've shown you how to Collapse a person. To Collapse an event, you simply personify it. Call it Mr. Illness, Ms. Financial Loss, Joe Fear, Susie Car Accident, or whatever, and follow the same steps outlined in Chapter 9. Of course, the next one will soon be on its way . . . thank God!

Collapsing One's Perceptions

Most people don't even consider the possibility that nothing is missing from their lives. If I'm traveling around the world and my children are in Houston and my wife is in New York, I have two options. I can fill out The Quantum Collapse Process form and enter into a state of gratitude and love and feel their presence, feel them in my heart, and carry them around with me no matter where I am in space-time, or I can go out of my heart and feel loss when I don't see their forms. If I'm wise and look carefully around me wherever I am, I can find every single one of the character traits that represent my wife or children to me. I can feel their presence around me throughout the day.

You're probably thinking, *Well, that's not the same.* Yes it is, if you Collapse it down in incredible detail. I do this almost every day with people, and I assure you that it's true. Look for infinite detail, and your loved ones are always with you. Do you know how that affects my experience as I travel around the world? I feel that I'm living in a giant house called "Planet Earth," and my wife and children are just in another room of my house. The only difference is that instead of walking from one room to another in my big house, I fly. It's all a game of perception. If I didn't have the ability to Collapse my perceptions and be with my loved ones in this fashion, I might not have been able to fulfill the destiny I saw in my vision so many years ago. Nothing is missing.

Long ago in India, a man thought he would like to embark upon the spiritual path and come to know God. As he walked along a river bank one day, he saw a *sadhu,* a holy man, seated in meditation beside the flowing water. He thought, *Ah, that is the one I have been looking for! I will ask him to teach me about God.* As he approached and began to bow in respect, the man suddenly leapt to his feet, seized him around the neck, dragged him into the river, and thrust his head below the surface. At first he struggled in shock, but then he thought to himself, *His wisdom already understands my quest, and this is a ritual purification. How wonderful!* and he relaxed.

As the immersion continued, he first thought that he must be very unworthy to require so much cleansing. When his breath began to run out, he became worried, but decided it was a clever test of his commitment and resolved to persevere. Eventually he had no air left. The iron grip on his neck didn't lessen an iota, and finally he thought, *This is not a holy man; he's a madman and means to drown me!* He began to struggle wildly, but his strength was soon exhausted and he became still.

The instant he ceased struggling, he was dragged from the water onto the river bank, where he lay, drawing in great shuddering gasps of air. When he'd recovered, the holy man fixed him with a penetrating gaze and asked, "What were you thinking about right there at the end?"

The man replied, "All I could think about was how much I wanted air."

"Come back to me when you want God that much, and I will teach you."

Divine Perfection

I read Leibniz's views on divine perfection when I was 18 years old, and he helped awaken a hunger in me to find for myself what he had seen. I had tears in my eyes without knowing why, because I didn't understand it as I do now, but I sensed a profound wisdom and a truth being revealed to me when I read, "There is divine perfection."

In his genius, Leibniz crossed a chasm of understanding and had a glimpse of divine order. Thousands of insights suddenly correlated, and his polarities of judgment on the universe came spontaneously to balance. He saw what I'm sharing with you, and in that awareness, he wrote about divine perfection. Once you've experienced The Quantum Collapse Process, you'll begin to know how to look for the other side of events. The glimpse of perfect equilibrium and light will birth a magnetism and potential energy in you that you won't ever lose.

It's like stretching a rubber band so far that it won't shrink back. My objective is to help you reach that point, because when you do, it's your turn to pass the lighted torch. You then have an inner motivation where your soul's wisdom is greater than anything someone else could teach you. You may use teachers to save time along your journey, but you won't depend only upon them because your spirit is awakened. Your heart is wiser than your intellect regarding human duality. It knows and feels the divine order, and it's humble enough to ask your soul for guidance.

The lies of reality show us exaggerations and minimizations of true actuality, which I define as this divine perfection, as perfectly balanced in all things. I continually hear people say in seminars and airports and everywhere I go, "Well, we're not perfect; we're just human. I'm not perfect; what do you expect?" They're comparing themselves to a one-sided idealism that they think is perfect, and as long as they live in and compare themselves to that illusion, they can never experience true divine perfection. Even their idea of heaven is often elusive, so if they were to get there, it would be another illusion and they would find imperfection there, too.

I say we already *are* perfection. The balance of both sides is itself the perfection, and we can't ever get away from it. If we really embrace and realize this, an amazing spiritual potentiality is birthed. We already are the perfection, and all we're doing is waking up to the balanced perfection that already exists.

That's why I say that no matter what you've done or not done, you're worthy of love. No matter what you've done or not done, it's divine perfection. If you could truly comprehend and deeply meditate on that, and go and explore the world with that state of knowing, you'd live in total humility to the Intelligence that governs us. You would then reach a point that Einstein, Newton, Dante, and Leibniz were talking about, and jump across the chasm and be graced by the divine order that is forever there.

In that state of grace is an unbounded potentiality of energy that is unfathomable to the average human mind, but attainable by the human psyche. When we occasionally break through the reality we live in and have glimpses of the heart and understand divine order, we wonder why we ever left that state. However, the evolutionary sequence maintains us on a journey of constantly moving outside it, in order to go in it. That's what evolution demands, consuming ever-greater illusions to birth increasing wisdom.

Since the age of 17, I've been studying the lives of people who have left immortal effects in history, people of greatness who have made major impacts and paradigm shifts in the world, in all fields. No matter which field they chose to master, these great geniuses displayed certain common character traits. They all trusted their inner vision and voice, which helped them see and hear what others seemed to pass by. They were confronted along their path by tremendous challenges, which they overcame through determination. They also knew the direction in which they were going.

The individuals who allow the voices on the inside to be louder than all the voices on the outside are the ones who step beyond the boundaries of what is considered possible, and leave the next immortal mark. To the degree that we listen to the immortal part of ourselves, our own soul and heart, we, too, can leave an immortal impact on this world. It's not because we choose or even care to; it's just the natural expression of those people who listen to their hearts and obey their souls.

I've been told many times, "You can't do some things," or "You're crazy or stupid," or "That's ridiculous or impossible." All that means is that the speaker doesn't think the task can be accomplished. Running a four-minute mile, stepping foot on the moon, talking to someone around the world at the speed of light, breaking the sound barrier—most of humankind's greatest accomplishments were once thought impossible.

> *"Many of life's failures are people who did not realize*
> *how close they were to success when they gave up."*
> — Thomas Edison

Whether they were artists, astronomers, theologians, or philosophers, the people who became immortal were the ones who were willing to do things that most people wouldn't dare to try. They didn't listen to what people said; they listened to their hearts. It doesn't matter if you're afraid. Everybody who ever did anything extraordinary was frightened at times. All things are in balance. If you have great fear, you also have great courage, for they remain in equal proportions; and both are necessary for us to evolve and grow.

Napoleon Hill

I once spoke on manifesting dreams at a prestigious Houston breakfast club. At the end of my address, an elderly gentleman came up to thank me and asked if he could take me to lunch. He wanted my advice on something, so about a week later, we met and he asked me for some insights on how to publish a book he'd planned to write for a long time. I shared with him what I knew, and he thanked me for the guidance, then he asked what else I did. I told him about The Breakthrough Experience, and he was intrigued. Two weeks later, he called my office and registered for the program. When he arrived, he introduced himself to the group. He had a very impressive manner, and was obviously a well-respected and influential man. He was one of those people who just seem to radiate self-determination and certainty.

During most of The Breakthrough Experience, he was polite, attentive, and present. He had a powerful experience when he finished his Collapse and opened his heart, and the next day, when we discussed the Materialization Formula, he was moved to tears. He had remembered something that had happened in his life, and put up his hand and asked if he could speak. There were about 15 people seated around the boardroom table, and he stood up, leaned forward with his hands on the table, and gazed steadily at each person in turn. Then he spoke.

He said, "Please don't underestimate the power of what Dr. Demartini is teaching; it is beyond what you can imagine right now. Forty years ago, I attended a seminar almost identical to this one, although of course there was no Collapse Process at that time, but many of the principles were there. Forty years ago, I was in a room very like this one with Napoleon Hill, and he taught us to decide our chief aim or purpose in life. He had us write down our dreams, goals, visions, and objectives, our affirmations or auto-suggestions, just as you have done here today. He also taught us the power and importance of visualizing and thinking clearly, and 40 years ago, I wrote down my dreams and goals. I put my life's mission down on paper."

At that moment, he pulled out his wallet and showed us a 40-year-old piece of paper wrapped in many layers of yellowed cellophane tape. He told us that his dreams were to become a multimillionaire before the age of 40, to have a beautiful home in the wealthiest part of the city, to own a company with more than 1,000 employees, and to drive a Mercedes. He wanted to marry the woman of his dreams, the winner of a state beauty contest, and have a son and a daughter with his dream lady. He wanted to become the headmaster of his alma mater, and to have prestige and honor in his city for all the things he had accomplished in his life. Last, he wanted to become an author and publish a book on how to turn mom-and-pop operations into major corporations.

He said, "Forty years ago, I wrote down these dreams and I followed what Napoleon Hill told me to do, which is virtually identical to Dr. Demartini's Materialization Formula. I can now say that I *did* become a multimillionaire before the age of 40, I *did* have a corporation with 1,000 employees, I *did* marry the beautiful woman of my dreams and we have two wonderful grown children. I drive a Mercedes, I became the headmaster of my university and am honored in my city. I accomplished every single one of the goals on my list, except one. When I met Dr. Demartini a few weeks ago, I realized that he was the key to the last of my goals, writing the book I'd always dreamed about.

"I had hesitated on that one for many years because when I stopped work in my 40s, I began spending a lot of time at the golf course, and I watched the men and women who had retired begin to die off. They lost their dreams, they lost their hearts, and they died. What I saw made me resist completing my goals because I was afraid the same thing would happen to me, but for some reason when I met Dr. Demartini and heard about his course, I knew that it was time for me to complete the last step.

"I tell you all this not to boast about my accomplishments, not for pride's sake, but to acknowledge the power and significance of the words that Dr. Demartini has spoken here these last two days. I'm living the very dreams I described 40 years ago by writing them down, and if you follow his instructions, you will stand up one day in the future and tell others just what I'm saying to you. The reason I share this with you now is because here is the finished book, after 40 years," and he gave me a copy.

He said, "I feel extremely inspired right now because I'm 72 years old and I just wrote out my next 40 years' worth of goals here today. Thank you, Dr. Demartini," and he sat down.

That man committed himself to his dreams, and he took advantage of the opportunity that Napoleon Hill offered him, and his life appeared exactly as he had dreamed it. You're here not just for pleasure, not just for a joyride; you have a mission here on Earth. When you wake up to it, you will accomplish things that most mortals won't comprehend. They won't, because they don't allow themselves the true *power* to imagine it. They won't understand the drive and the depth of the motivation because they're living from the suicide-survival-security-social level, instead of from the spiritual self-actualization perspective.

A genius is one who listens to the guidance of their soul and obeys, and every human being in this world is a potential genius. Everyone we've ever met, no matter what they've done or not done, is a genius deep inside. It's our responsibility to identify and reflect that in them and ourselves, and when we do, they and we will unfold it. That has been my calling, and I believe that all human beings do have one.

In 1901, Dr. Richard Maurice Bucke published a book called *Cosmic Consciousness*. In it, he described the 43 most illuminated people in history, from Dante and Mohammed to Christ and the Buddha. One thing they all had in common was an inner voice with which they communed. Even Einstein used to commune with it daily. I could list hundreds of other names of great minds who listened to their inner voice and left their immortal effects on history. I wonder what would happen if *you* mastered the art of listening to yours today?

Sir Isaac Newton said, "I once sat for 17 days without rest, receiving ever-new glimpses and awakenings about the celestial motions of the heavenly bodies and the laws that govern them. I could not sleep. I would close my eyes for a moment and be illuminated with yet another vision." I believe that all of us are capable of living that type of inspiration.

You may be thinking, *Look, I just got a job, I'm looking for a partner, and I really don't have time to think about such things.* But just know that there's an immortal part of you that's destined for greatness, and sooner or later it will have its day.

The Breakthrough Experience and The Quantum Collapse Process can help you awaken your hidden inspirations and make an immortal difference. We're not mortal beings having occasional spiritual experiences. We're immortal beings having a brief mortal experience. That's the actual truth hidden behind all of our mortal perceptions.

All my adult life, I've dreamed of passing on to others this immortal torch about the magnificent divine perfection because I knew that if great beings could share it with me, I could certainly share it with others. I know that through my speaking, books, audios, videos, CDs, and other media outlets, I've been blessed to be able to touch hundreds of millions of people. The more I can share this message, the more the wisdom of divine love and light spreads.

I hope I've inspired you and seeded within you the essence of what your heart has been revealing all along. You're an immortal genius with a profound destiny. You live in a magnificent universe where divine order reigns. Nothing is missing. Every moment of your existence is a precious gift. You're surrounded by love every instant of your life. I hope these seeds take root in your heart and you make them immortal. Honor every single thing that happens in your life. Take the time to find divinity in every fragment of space and time. Consider this your personal mission, because the most honorable thing a human being can do is to say thank you to life.

I say, "Where is God *not?*" and any place that I don't see divinity, I can't see my *life*. Think about this: If there is a Creator, what did that Being create the universe from? There wasn't anything here before, so it must all have been created from the substance of the Creator Itself. So what are you? You are a tiny piece of the body of God. May you forever love so you may live up to it.

Your Last 24 Hours, and Your Obituary

To more fully love yourself and others, it helps to have a life filled with meaning and purpose, where you know why you're really here. Having a purpose provides focus, courage, and the certainty to face and break through your fears. Feeling like you're fulfilling your destiny provides a tremendous source of self-worth and adds meaning to every day.

What follows are two final exercises designed to help you find out what's truly important to you. If you take them seriously, the rewards can be profound.

Exercise 1

If you knew you only had 24 hours to live, how would you spend your remaining time? What would you do and say?

_____

_____

_____

_____

_____

_____

_____

_____

_____

_____

I've taken thousands of people through this exercise, and virtually every one of them said they would tell the people in their lives how much they loved and appreciated them. When you have only 24 hours to live, you focus on your highest priorities. Expressing love and gratitude appears to be every human being's highest priority. Since you don't know when your last 24 hours is, what are you waiting for?

Exercise 2

Write your own obituary. This is to be spoken at your funeral, and you can imagine it written either by yourself or by someone who loves you. Write one obituary for the life you have lived so far, as if you were to die at the end of these 24 hours; and the second obituary for the life you would love to have lived, one where you fulfilled all of your goals and lived fully and gratefully with purpose and meaning. Compare the two and ask yourself which life inspires you most.

Your Obituary #1:

_____

_____

_____

_____

_____

_____

_____

_____

_____

Your Obituary #2

_____

_____

_____

_____

_____

_____

_____

One of your two personas may have written your obituary, or you may have written it directly from your heart. Your self-righteous persona would say things such as, "She was always a good person, she was never cruel to anyone, and she was always generous and nice." Your self-wrongeous persona would say things such as, "She apologizes to everyone for her shortcomings and regrets that she could not have been more considerate of others." Your obituary will reflect the way you feel about yourself and your life: positive, negative, or loving.

Life is precious, and we sometimes forget that. If you truly allow yourself to make these exercises real, they will motivate you.

Thank you for allowing me to share my heart with you on this journey. May we meet and break bread together one day in the future. Know this to be true: When you have love, you see love; when you live greatness, you're surrounded by nothing but greatness; and every single human being has love and greatness inside them just waiting for the day it can come out and shine. May this book bring that day closer for you.

The Ten Daily Pillars of Wisdom

Below are my Ten Daily Pillars of Wisdom.
Use them for daily contemplation and action.

1. Inspired Action
2. Loving Service
3. Grateful Prayer
4. Divine Guidance
5. Sharing Wisdom
6. Caring Sincerely
7. Silent Presence
8. Studying Truths
9. Temperate Rhythm
10. Fair Exchange

Thank you for journeying with me through
The Breakthrough Experience.

— Dr. John F. Demartini

Notes

Notes

Notes

Notes

Notes

About the Author

Dr. John F. Demartini, founder of the Concourse of Wisdom School of Philosophy of Healing, is a rare and gifted man whose span of experience and study encompasses broad scopes of knowledge. He began his career as a doctor of chiropractic and went on to explore more than 200 different disciplines in pursuit of what he calls Universal Principles of Life and Health. As an international speaker, Dr. Demartini breathes new life into his audiences with his enlightening perspectives, humorous observations of human nature, and practical action steps. His words of wisdom inspire minds, open hearts, and motivate people into action. His philosophy and revolutionary understanding of the power of unconditional love is reshaping psychology as we know it, and his revolutionary personal transformation methodologies are transforming the lives of millions of people all over the world.

If you'd like information on attending *The Breakthrough Experience*™ or consulting with Dr. Demartini to experience *The Quantum Collapse Process*™, contact Dr. Demartini's Concourse of Wisdom Headquarters at:

Dr. John F. Demartini
2800 Post Oak Blvd., #5250
Houston, TX 77056

Toll-free: 888-DEMARTINI • Phone: 713-850-1234
Fax: 713-850-9239
www.drdemartini.com   **info@drdemartini.com**

We hope you enjoyed this Hay House book. If you'd like to receive a free catalog featuring additional Hay House books and products, or if you'd like information about the Hay Foundation, please contact:

Hay House, Inc.
P.O. Box 5100
Carlsbad, CA 92018-5100

(760) 431-7695 or **(800) 654-5126**
(760) 431-6948 (fax) or **(800) 650-5115 (fax)**
www.hayhouse.com® • **www.hayfoundation.org**

Published and distributed in Australia by: Hay House Australia Pty. Ltd., 18/36 Ralph St., Alexandria NSW 2015 • *Phone:* 612-9669-4299 • *Fax:* 612-9669-4144
www.hayhouse.com.au

Published and distributed in the United Kingdom by: Hay House UK, Ltd., 292B Kensal Rd., London W10 5BE • *Phone:* 44-20-8962-1230 • *Fax:* 44-20-8962-1239
www.hayhouse.co.uk

Published and distributed in the Republic of South Africa by: Hay House SA (Pty), Ltd., P.O. Box 990, Witkoppen 2068 • *Phone/Fax:* 27-11-706-6612 • orders@psdprom.co.za

Published in India by: Hay House Publications (India) Pvt. Ltd., Muskaan Complex, Plot No. 3, B-2, Vasant Kunj, New Delhi 110 070 • *Phone:* 91-11-4176-1620 • *Fax:* 91-11-4176-1630 www.hayhouseindia.co.in

Distributed in Canada by: Raincoast , 9050 Shaughnessy St., Vancouver, B.C. V6P 6E5
Phone: (604) 323-7100 • *Fax:* (604) 323-2600 • www.raincoast.com

Tune in to **HayHouseRadio.com**® for the best in inspirational talk radio featuring top Hay House authors! And, sign up via the Hay House USA Website to receive the Hay House online newsletter and stay informed about what's going on with your favorite authors. You'll receive bimonthly announcements about: Discounts and Offers, Special Events, Product Highlights, Free Excerpts, Giveaways, and more!
www.hayhouse.com®